For Robert, with love,

the fruit of a labor he started years ago.

Toni.

D1564200

Becoming What One Is

Becoming What One Is

AUSTIN WARREN

ANN ARBOR

THE UNIVERSITY OF MICHIGAN PRESS

Copyright © by the University of Michigan 1995
Published in the United States of America by
The University of Michigan Press
Manufactured in the United States of America
⊖ Printed on acid-free paper
1998 1997 1996 1995   4 3 2 1

A CIP catalogue record for this book is available from the British Library.

Library of Congress Cataloging-in-Publication Data

Warren, Austin, 1899–1986.
  Becoming what one is / Austin Warren.
     p.   cm.
  ISBN 0-472-10287-7 (alk. paper)
  1. Warren, Austin, 1899–1986. 2. Critics—United States—
Biography. 3. Biographers—United States—Biography. 4. English
teachers—United States—Biography. I. Title.
PN75.W3A3   1995
809—dc20
  [B]   94-48110
                                                          CIP

I wish to express my thanks to Robert Kent, who read and edited this
manuscript, faithfully following Mr. Warren's wishes.

                                                        Toni Warren

For Toni

wise critic of this book and
loving sustainer of its author

Foreword

Russell Fraser

Good poets are less rare than competent practitioners of the critic's job of work, and Austin Warren is one of the latter. Part of that interlocking directorate of high-toned men of letters between the two World Wars and after—they found house room in quarterlies like the *Kenyon, Sewanee,* and *Southern* reviews—he helped make our criticism an art form. The life, touched with greatness, mirrors the art, not always true of writers, and publication of his memoir, *Becoming What One Is,* will confirm this. Friends who knew him for a long time still salute the greatness. A passionate consensus, it needs inquiring into, now that he is dead and the matter-of-fact all recorded.

"Brother Austin," Allen Tate called him, a joke meant in earnest. Austin himself initiated this mode of address, applied to friends in the confraternity he presided over as abbot. The friends were Brother Cleanth, Sister Tinkum (Mrs. Cleanth Brooks), Brother Allen. A new essay by T. S. Eliot was an encyclical. It needed exegesis, and meeting the need he headed his letters from "The Oratory of SS. Basil and Gregory Nazienzen," not a made-up place, the chapel in his house in Ann Arbor. Leon Edel remembered the chapel, a dim recess, icons on a low table draped with an altar cloth. The first time I called on Austin, summoned to the stone house on E. University near campus, I took the highball he handed me and plunked it down on his altar. Our budding friendship almost ended right there.

It began in the 1960s, when I came to Michigan—he would have said and did say when I got the "call," not a phone call. In this academic venue where they laid out the "corpus" of letters, he showed like bright metal on a sullen ground. He cared about poetry, rare in English departments, and spoke without embarrassment of prayer. "Tomorrow is the Feast of Corpus Christi; pray for me."

The Eastern saints and icons locate him in his Greek Orthodox phase, among the varieties of religious experience that went to form an American original. He liked "heart-religion," also controverting the finer points of divinity, sport for a thinking man. The Methodist Christianity he got from his parents, only a higher prudence, "offered little to stir the imagination of the young"—I am quoting from his life of Henry James the Elder, like many biographies a version of its author—and failed altogether to quicken "the impulse to high deed and self-forgetful purpose." So in his teens he became a "Jesus freak," then a Swedenborgian who detected connections between the soul and the natural kingdom. In adulthood, carrying this baggage with him, he joined the Anglican Church. A village librarian he knew, "of sharp mind and sharper tongue," claimed the right to shift her pew from the Congregational church to the Episcopalian when the counsels of either displeased her, and this crotchety woman gives Austin's likeness too.

He mustn't be thought of as eclectic, however—magpies are that—and whatever the nomenclature, owed allegiance to a single religion. His laid hold "upon the heart, upon life," both terms asking attention. Beginning at home but self-forgetful, the religion he practiced meditated high deeds and didn't bring peace but a sword. It didn't pull a long face either. "John the Baptist with a sense of humor," he called James the Elder, a minatory prophet who hectored the rest of us, warning that the Day of the Lord was at hand. But his prophecies, like Austin's, were not less insistent "for the jocular idiom," or you could put this the other way round.

The autobiography, taking him up to his fortieth year, "nel mezzo del cammin," suggests his special quality, vintage New England filtered through other places, some exotic. An education-of-the-hero book, this account of gearing up resembles Milton's at Horton but isn't all "pre-'Lycidas,'" and before you finish a modern hero comes into his own. Self-made, he forged his soul when others weren't looking. Yankees did for themselves, and his birth on the Fourth of July—pinpointing the time, he said it occurred while the village parade was passing—chimed with his independent spirit. Anyway, this Swedenborgian saw a "correspondence."

His early unloved youth tried him in a crucible he could have dispensed with. On the farm at Stow, his father coped "variously," his mother kept her distance, but he got along with the cows. No soul mates smoothed his way and some persecutors blocked it, like the local bully who beat him up at school. One of his teachers, "utterly, painfully, New Englandly conscientious," made him hate Shakespeare, not easy. The plays, said Austin ruefully, helped you parse old English words. Wesleyan College, entered by him without expectations, didn't disappoint. Hiding out in the library, he instructed himself, though.

He didn't always elude academic tormentors, and later, at Harvard, awful G. L. Kittredge jumped him through hoops. Irving Babbitt at Harvard ("my one great 'official' teacher") spoke to him where he lived, or where one part of him did, and he warmed to Babbitt, and Paul Elmer More at Princeton. But these mentors and friends set snares for his feet. Both wanted disciples in the narrow church they belonged to, and, "becoming what one is," he had to fight free of them both.

Searching for a vocation, he turned inevitably to teaching, his appointed role, and in his twenties recreated Little Gidding in rural New England. This was "the place you would be likely to come from" (remembering Eliot in *The Four Quartets*). An Arnoldian saving remnant, St. Peter's School admitted only the "elect." Like Austin's chapel in Michigan, it existed in time and space, "in eternity and ubiquity" too. Not everybody talks the way he did.

"Oral glibness," his own, often fooled him, however, and he needed pen and paper to show up "my incoherences." He said you couldn't be an honest teacher without finding time to write. (Facile proponents of "great" teaching unmediated by writing didn't hear him and still don't.) "To be, or to do, anything," you had to "give up almost everything," though, and his younger time shows him jettisoning cargo. A rigorous scholar himself, he looked mistrustfully at Professor X, "master of a single theme or the exposition of a single dead author—a life for a life." Right on target, that last bit, scathing talk from someone who earned it.

Disputing the received wisdom—it was all for pigeonholes—he wanted to be *ad omnia paratus*, "writing about what he was interested in writing about, and in whatever mode." This led to the study of comparative literature, an academic heresy still over the horizon when he got started. He "had the nerve to conceive of it" (said his friend Glauco Cambon) "as the normal horizon of critical inquiry," not another special "field" to be marked out and properly tagged. Once he told me, "You are a comparativist," adding, as he was. I cherish the likeness.

In the 1930s, throwing away the 3-by-5 cards, he set up as a critic. Next he dropped the formal lectures, turning his classroom into a happening. A scandal to the scribes, he asked students to close their notebooks and open their minds. In the photo on my office wall he stands silent before the class, lips pursed, eyes abstracted behind the thick glasses. This professor is evidently at sea. Much risk in letting them know that you don't know the answers, and most, dreading silence, fill it with words, words. A caption beneath the photo has Austin saying, however: "I want, in a sense, to teach something which I have not yet learned."

As this story ends, he has found his vocation, teaching the young who committed themselves to his "pastoral" care—that was how he put it—and reflecting in print on what he taught them. Twin pursuits, they kept him busy the rest of his life.

The reflections move him a long way from his master Babbitt and the Neo-Humanist ensign he nailed to the mast. (Fluttering bravely, it went down with the ship.) A moralistic creed, Neo-Humanism held that our modern "decadence" represented a sad falling off. Rousseau, a famous decadent, laid the ax to our tree, but already you could see the rot setting in with Shakespeare. His *Antony and Cleopatra* balanced good and evil in too perfect an equipoise, like the swan's down feather lackeying the tide. Babbitt wished it would stick in one place.

Accommodating what the master called perverse or morbid, Austin made his own larger and scarier world. Or rather he lived it, exemplifying, said Philip Young, the baroque in the flesh, "dramatic, jagged, genuine." Near the end of his life, he still found life complex, intolerably this, and kept trying to simplify in the interest of a harmony he knew in his bones was factitious. But ecumenicism, the real right catholic thing, forbade him to throw out the baby with the bathwater. "*Any* of the babies," he said.

His tolerance, different from Laodiceanism where you don't speak your mind, not having one or not giving a damn, begins with the scrupulous canvasing of fact. So many facts or figures in the carpet must postpone a rush to judgment, but first of all you have to entertain them. For the literary critic, Austin par excellence, this meant absorption in words. A "lay theologian" (self-styled), he got his finicking preoccupation with words from teasing out occulted meanings in the Bible. The same myopic queerness—a vice, Dr. Johnson thought—describes Shakespeare.

Biblical exegesis, "the archetype of our literary 'close reading,'" flowered, Austin said, in hermeneutics, a science of the interpretation of texts. He saw how this science played into the "New Critical" study of literature, and I see him myself as an etymologist, though raised to the nth power, with connections to Ransom, Blackmur, and Tate. Among his antecedents is the early Christian exegete, Isidore of Seville. He wrote an *Etymologies* too.

Dusted off in recent days, hermeneutics, new style, is one of modern theory's buzzwords, and gives an infinite range of meanings their charter. Purporting to deal with poetry, it pirouettes about the poem, doing what it can to keep from closing with the thing itself. Fear inspirits its little dance, possibly hatred, the fear at any rate having grounds. Words "slip, slide, perish, / Decay with imprecision," and getting them right is work for intellectual athletes. Sometimes old Isidore, grappling with words, burned his fingers.

But hermeneutics in its accepted sense, while it allows of multiple meanings—and how should it not, truth being in the cards—stipulates their finite character. For determining the range, artistic intention is the sine qua non. Often ambiguous, this gleam in the artist's eye isn't unknowable, but the reader who hopes to spot it must keep his own eyes on the page. He isn't all-in-all sufficient ("The Critic as Artist"), and *id est* is how he deals with the text.

Readers in our time, when literary criticism, freed of its tether, runs downhill like the Gadarene swine, will find it useful to look into Austin Warren. Close reading is his benchmark, meaning honesty, meaning infinite patience, and of course he became a New Critic. Reared to his shame by ideological critics (he confessed to Blackmur in a letter of 1940), he said how "in the last five years, my association with poets and my own dissatisfaction at so external a way of dealing with poetry"—sociology and all that—"have turned me to very different methods." Nowadays his own teaching was largely in the spirit of *Understanding Poetry*, Brooks's and R. P. Warren's manifesto to the classroom. These preceptors and their New Critical colleagues took the line from St. John's Gospel for their point of departure. "In the beginning was the Word."

Theory of Literature (1942), the influential primer Austin made with René Wellek, displays his different methodology, not an ideologue's but pragmatic. More than any other work, said Allen Tate, it civilized the teaching of literature. "Wellek & Warren" stated the obvious, rather like the Declaration of Independence. E.g., "The natural and sensible starting-point for work in literary scholarship is the interpretation and analysis of the works of literature themselves." To beneficiaries after the fact, it sounds ipso facto, but fifty years ago brought down the house of index cards. Today when old corruptions titivated with new labels are back in the market, the obvious truth needs restating.

Only the works, said these urbane revolutionaries, "justify all our interest in the life of an author, in his social environment and the whole process of literature." Professors of literature, hunting ideas, preferred an all-around-the-barn mode of study, however. Students, hungry sheep who looked up but weren't fed, paid the price for this. "Confronted with the task of actually analysing and evaluating a work of art," they didn't know where to begin.

Yes, and I still get red in the face, remembering the first time I tried. *Sa vie et son oeuvre* gave the sense of Eng Lit when I went to school, and anecdotes, some entertaining, set the poet before us. Or Professor X, consulting his Tillyard, filled in the cultural "surround." Background was foreground, and if you believed him, unlocked the heart of the mystery. Nobody explicated the text.

Theory of Literature changed all that. But it didn't propose that we read in a vacuum, the vulgar canard detractors lay at New Criticism's door. Ignorant of the significant past, American college graduates—a sorry bunch, Austin thought—forfeited "their proffered share in civilization." He and friends meant to reclaim it. Blackmur and Burke, two of the friends, knew more of our inheritance than any Ph.D. But they knew it on their pulses, and inert knowledge didn't suffice them.

Meanwhile, Professor X guarded the portals. Easy to dismiss him, a woolgatherer and so on. Chomping on his cigar, he looked endearing. But his bite was worse than his bark. At worst a "bookful blockhead," at best an appreciator who appealed to the viscera, he lacked the critical faculty, so forgot the original motive of knowing. What was that? Austin asked (in an essay mediating between the scholar and critic), and answered: to understand and apply. You see how his religion, personal plus social, dictates his critical stance.

Canonizing knowledge, he said the critic without background can never transcend journalism. "But without consciousness of a foreground in which men live and act he remains an *érudit*." So down with "disjecta membra," eye against hand and hand against heart. This New Critic has a watchword: "only connect."

Style enforced the connections, a point lost on primitivists who cry up the naked truth. "Plain, simple, sullen," Donne called this truth, indifferent to the niceties of language and unaware that nice isn't pretty but exact. Belletristic critics, the other face of a bad coin, thought a feast of language was better than enough. "Strike out every other sentence," Austin told them. Like Henry James (the Younger), he meant to cut off all "gracious twaddle."

Boiling down suited him, and the essay, not the book, is the form most in tune with his genius. Inscribing a copy of *The Elder Henry James* to Leon Edel, he said he longed to free this early work from verbosity, reducing the whole "to an immaculate 125 pages." He wanted only the essence, chapters condensed to paragraphs, paragraphs to a sentence. Each was a "topic sentence." Plunging straight in, he omitted the formal preface and ended without that conventional summary, dear to "Thus we see" writers. But he didn't appeal to *nuda veritas*, no such animal, and another impulse opposes this centripetal one. He wanted his essays readable, not only about literature "but themselves literature." This second clause bespeaks a man with pretensions.

A mandarin of style, he cosseted words more than clarity needed, and that was New Critical too. His style, different from Blackmur's, convoluted, sometimes affected, edges toward the academy, like Tate's and Ransom's, all three university trained. But all have in common an uncanny sense of words as almost corporal entities. Being alive where the intellectual "message" is only matter-of-fact, they make a rival creation. More and more, this greatly aspiring writer came to see that the kind of meaning he aimed at, going beyond communication, incarnated itself in style: "and it is style—meaning in diction and rhythm—which is my final concern." Note the rhythm, important. Prose writers, those who matter, don't number syllables but not less than poets have a pattern before them, and the music counts as much as what they "say."

Not a critic by default (a failed poet or novelist) and unashamed of his profession, Austin called himself some kind of artist. "I would rather be a doorkeeper in the house of art than to dwell, all confidently and smilingly and blandly, in the courts of erudition and commerce." His friend Wallace Fowlie is putting words in his mouth. The words are stirring but don't claim enough for this humble yet proud man, and in the last chapter of the autobiography, "Becoming a Writer," he elevated his sights.

Though skilled in "practical criticism" where the self-effacing critic plays second fiddle to the artist, he found it easy "to slip into the view that novels exist in order that they may receive expert treatment; that poems exist in order that they may be interpreted." Then, flooring us, he says: "If fin de siècle poets could feel that the

final end of the world is that it may all be taken up and consummated in a poem, I may be tempted to the view that the poem, in
turn, is to be consummated by its absorption into a critical essay."
The superbity astonishes—he himself feels its force and acknowl-
edges a temptation that common sense will want to correct. However, the truth is out and stamps him a son of Oscar, after all the
Critic as Artist. If I contradict myself in this portrait of him, then
I contradict myself, and plead only that I take my lead from him.

Like his life of James the Elder, his own biography "is properly and
primarily that of a mind." But the mind, a house of many man-
sions, resists classification. He said of his hero and might have said
of himself that his "independence, wit, and piquant idiom served
to make him a subject for anecdotes." Over the years the anecdotes
proliferated, some piquant like the idiom. They don't set him
clear, though, and to express what he called "my stance" you need
an oxymoron, the rhetorical term he learned from his study of the
baroque sensibility. Illustrating, he drew his own ambiguous portrait: "an aristocratic noun or verb qualified but not wholly negated
by its accompanying democratizing adjective or adverb!"

Fastidious in person, this aesthete walled off the world he
lived in with books, music, and high talk. He had a rich baritone
and kept and played a reed organ, his music, said Jack Wheelwright, "sprinkling silence over sound." A primitivist he wasn't,
and while at St. Peter's School thought of taking lessons in singing
and dance. His letters, sometimes precious, favor inverted com-
mas. One, Henry Jamesian, tells of having "made an effort at
'games.'" Neologisms cast him down, *realtor* for *real estate agent*.
He wrote a crabbed hand but wouldn't type his letters and wondered a little if you did. The typewriter intervened between friends.

No good himself at driving a car or cooking a meal, he thought
teachers ought to cook and work with their hands. At St. Peter's,
modeled on Brook Farm, they did this. He was the dean and saw
to it. Religious but no quietist, he instructed his flock that politics
and religion were "central modes of existential life." Grave but no
Puritan, like the elder James he relished what the world had to
offer: "good cigars, oysters, smart tailoring, books." Not a toper,
he liked his drink, preferring dry martinis. Kenneth Burke recalled
the two of them, arguing all night as they walked the dirt roads
around Andover, New Jersey, breaking off for "alcoholic replenish-
ment."

A generous critic, he was Chaucer's Clerk, fortified, said Edel, by an artist's discipline. Opening himself to friends who were writers, he corrected their prose in his great soft black pencil. Sometimes the Clerk was Cato the Censor, whose comments in the margin made you pale. "Mine is an irenic spirit," he asserted, but the peace-loving man had his swingeing side. If you crossed him he smote you. He had an aura too, adding cubits to his stature, also a large bump of ego. Woe to the friend who presumed.

Abasing himself in a letter to Tate, he said we were all "poor, ignorant, sinful, lost, wavering and wandering creatures." Some wandered more than others, however. He wondered at Blackmur, the autodidact who never made it out of high school. He himself was Dr. Warren, a Princeton Ph.D. Though disdaining academic credentials, he was willing to have it both ways.

"Literature *as such*" made a war cry or party shibboleth on the Wellek and Warren side, an Iowa colleague remembered, and Austin, fixated on the figure in the carpet, comes close in his criticism to venerating art for its own sake. He wrote, however: "I distinctly do not believe that literature *alone* or *as such* is adequate for the salvation of mankind." "Our Jamesian traveler of the mind"—an apt phrase of Cambon's—wasn't about to succumb to Gilbert Osmond's temptation. Chasing salvation, he is the highest type of political man, i.e., engagé, and though harking back to the 1890s, differs profoundly from ancestors like Pater. "In me, from the start, have existed an artist (or at least an aesthete)," he said, "along with a moralist." Though the moralist was "sternest in self-judgment," that didn't preclude judging others. Cain's chilly question: "Am I my brother's keeper?" would have seemed rhetorical to him.

"Our business," said his friend Jack Wheelwright, was "minding other people's." Like Old Testament Seth in Wheelwright's poem, Austin made wars to found or reconstitute the city wrecked by Cain. Alert to ends where most, missing the Pisgah-sight, care only for means, he undertook to see that we didn't board the wrong train for Beulah. "It may land you up in Englewood, New Jersey." Implacably serious, hence seriocomic, he raises eyebrows like Don Quixote. But he moves you to wonder, like Hamlet and Lear. In a world where all are on the make or take, he is our polestar.

No man more conservative (as all must be who hope to save for the future the best of the past). Preserving his ties to church, university, and political state, he stayed in partly from "a steady faith in the importance of continuity." Skepticism fueled this faith, a perception that the evils of institutions, part and parcel of the nature of the beast, weren't "to be abolished by substituting a new set of institutions." But he wrote himself a socialist, more exactly "an orthodoxly-religious-politically-socialist man." Elitist, at the same time an inveterate democrat, he set his face against the acquisitive society, like Hawthorne, the elder James, and John Brooks Wheelwright, heroes he celebrated, one of them a personal friend. This mixed bag was good company and he adds to its sum.

You can trace his line of descent from nineteenth-century utopians like long-forgotten Fourier, he of the "phalansteries," Bronson Alcott of Fruitlands, a socialistic community, and Welsh Robert Owen, who founded New Harmony in Indiana's green and pleasant land. Actuated by the same impulse as these benevolent reformers, he meant to establish the City of God on earth. Unlike them, he wasn't a behaviorist or cocksure environmentalist—too worldly wise for that—and hardly supposed that we could pull ourselves up by our bootstraps. Estimating the crack in the bowl, he understood how all last things lie outside the scope of reform. Over St. Peter's School the spirit of three "high rebels," Ruskin, Arnold, and Newman, hovered persistently. He said what they rebelled against was "progress."

Of his many books, the autobiography comes last, but it seems right to say that all the books are autobiographical, so many versions of an etymologist in touch with root or radical meanings. The life he finished in his retirement, cherished labor, has waited years on publication, too bad but not surprising. Whatever he wrote, said Cambon, restates "an underlying dissent from the established values of his society." It paid him back with silence. Society likes its heroes, if not compromised exactly, then willing to compromise, an Honest Abe who is only moderately this, a moderately pious Jesus Christ. He doesn't oblige.

"I still see him" (drawing here on the recollection of friends), smallish, brisk, neat in tweeds, a man for attachments but warmly distant, an informal man but mannerly, not slipshod, never that. With the ease that transcends etiquette went an elegant bearing, but even in age a touch of boyishness enlivened his face.

Good at listening, he heard you out, then said his own say with style, sensibility, and candor. Speaking, he put his head down, the dark bright eyes squinting with thought. But a mystic tropism drew up his handsome jaw, jutting higher and ever higher. Not a calculated performer, he didn't study his words for effect. On the other hand, he didn't open his shirt front. Ligatures weren't for him and he leaped without preamble from abstruse speculation to whimsical absurdities. Booming laughter acknowledged the absurdities, partly at his own expense.

Entering the classroom, he left preliminaries aside. Others introduced themselves, called the roll, looked at notes. Superior to notes or not having any, he took off his wristwatch, laid it down on the desk, then, lighting a cigarette, got going *in medias res.* Slight but tense on the podium, he hinted at latent energies, like a coiled spring. The spring was firmly under control, though.

Other views, withershins to this one, modify or amplify his image in the mind's eye. His teacher's job consumed him, and unself-conscious gyrations suggested to students that he lived on some higher plane, off by himself. He twitched, grimaced, shot his jaw up, putting his neck in peril, made sudden penetrations, tortured unlit cigarettes into tiny shreds. What the students thought seemed important to this master who was also a student, and questions needing answers kept them on the boil. Talk in his classroom, never *bavard*, was always to the center, the sacred text he held in his hand.

"Apostle to the midwest," he called himself, a whimsical characterization. Well-meaning accounts, making much of the apostleship, have him converting the heathen. Would that it were so, but in the nature of things he failed to convert them. Not that Michigan was less tractable than anyplace, USA. Out there in the world, though, it was all savage Boeotia.

Dear Joe Lee Davis, the best of the department in Austin's later days, evokes him at the Bull Ring, 111 West Huron Street, the "aristodemocracy" he organized in Ann Arbor. Who will forget those heady times when Warner Rice and Kenneth Burke "argued together at the bar over foaming steins while goggle-eyed graduate students drank in every word." Etc. This vignette, more poetry than truth, has its charm. Years after, Burke, back in town for a visit, encountered a survivor from the good old days. Boring them to death as ever but unmarked by time, he still watched before the portals of knowledge. There before Austin came on the scene, he ushered him out at the end. Recognizing Professor X, their immemorial antagonist, Burke couldn't remember his name.

Austin, said his wife Toni, "had ever felt an 'exile' in the Middle West," but flaneurs on either coast aren't to take comfort from a putdown. The sojourner for truth stood on the outside. Wherever he parked his bags, he existed in the university as a kind of fifth column or living reproach. "I belong," he said, with those "whose lot it is to live 'on the boundary.'" This neither-here-northere place left him open to all weathers, also to the ardors of parochial men who live under one flag.

In the 1950s a severe nervous breakdown laid him low; perhaps it enriched him. "Relief and release and emancipation," he called it. The same "'vastation' of strength and pride" overtook James the Elder, either breakdown or conversion. "It may be," Austin said, "that one is not obliged to choose between the two." He inclined toward the latter, believing that purgation precedes illumination. It doesn't seem likely that he meant to cheer us up or cheer himself up, as when heartless poets affirm that the best is yet to be, and I think this painful caesura, opening in the middle years, illuminated for him the provisionality of everything he stood for.

Toward the end, his labors met stony soil. Strength and eyesight failed, and the man who lived for his writing, addressed to the greater world, wrote letters, addressed to a few. They show him "moody, introspective, and self-distrustful," gripped by "a bleak and black state of depression." His autobiography, now about to go off in the mails a second time, hasn't wowed them in the courts of erudition and commerce, and he wonders whether "I have 'shot my bolt,' have lost my usefulness."

Retired in Providence, Rhode Island, a final way station, he regretted "that we live in such a barbarous age." He said it grew steadily worse. He wasn't an old man grousing and hadn't lost his taxonomer's eye. Bad ideas, long maturing, finally ripe, were the culprit. He lived to see the discrediting of his empirical faith, sapped by new theory, Platonizing and self-referential. Let us have no more of the Word made flesh, they said, inflamed by hatred of *terra damnata*. Where there used to be a text was a pool for Narcissus.

No one, said an old friend, felt more touched by the approval of his fellows than he. It didn't crown his last days, and this festered. However, he wrote: "We have to do our work, our 'thing,' *ohne Hast, ohne Rast.*" Applause or its absence weren't in it.

From the beginning, he cared little for prizes, even wages. At St. Peter's they never made a dime, all right with an eleemosynary man. "I want to seek those things which are, for me, their own rewards," he said in his thirties. Among the desired things, truth headed the list. He spent a lifetime pursuing it, though knowing a will-o'-the-wisp when he saw one. Not the goal but the search itself kept him going, however, and offered sufficient reward.

Preface

&❧

I undertake in this book an autobiography—that is, an interpretation of my life, based primarily on memory though checked by reference to my diaries and journals. I have worked within defined limits: I have not quoted from journals or letters. And I do not attempt to cover the whole of my life. Myself a constant reader of biographies and autobiographies, I see that, in the case of literary, intellectual, or spiritual men (the adjectives are not mutually exclusive), it is the formative years—*la jeunesse de*—which most engage: the volume entitled "The Obscure Years" or "The Untried Years," the period up to the first conscious or public success of the narrator. Thereafter we have chiefly the chronicle of his books or paintings or political triumphs: the person becomes merely the productive agent. But how did he *become* what he turned out to be?

It was my initial intention to narrate the story of my first thirty years; but I am a literary critic, not a poet, and I did not reach the end of my 'becoming' till I was forty, when I published my fourth book, the first I regard as truly realized, and when I left Boston, my cherished city, for the state universities of Iowa and Michigan; so I have extended my story by five chapters more.

I have had, I think, a rich life, in all its periods, a rich inner life of thought and feeling. It has been a life of seeking and finding. If I reread my journals, especially those of the 1930s, I seem to have been engaged chiefly in the search for identity, for which of my potential selves I should center on—a search for self-definition.

My two modes of self-discovery were writing—direct self-confrontation—and teaching, which meant to me the intermediation between the sacred texts of literature and the existential selves of the young men and women before me. The only kind of teaching which I cared for was the kind I saw illustrated in the work of a few really great teachers under whom I sat: this involved less the impartation of knowledge than the constant search for wisdom and the constant attempt to be oneself such a man of integrity—the same outside the classroom as in—as could in some measure exemplify the ideal of the humanities.

As the few theorists of the genre have seen, it is problematic what the stance of the autobiographer should be. He is writing of what is past; but is he seeking to recover the self he was at each period of the past, and what his motives, feelings, and perceptions then were, or is he interpreting all those former selves and periods from the point of view of his present self? To answer my own question: I have tried not to look ahead or to interpret the more distant past in terms of the more recent, but to reproduce my past selves and their accompanying feelings and judgments as accurately as I could. When I have felt obligated to add some present comment on the past, I have aimed to make the distinction clear. Though stylistically, in revising the whole, I have sought to achieve a relatively coherent and unified tone; I have sought, in so doing, not to blur or blend the stages of a developing self.

The prime subject of this book is constantly an Education; but that education was far from being merely bookish or academic or conceptual: it was much more basically aesthetic, social, moral, and spiritual.

Austin Warren
Providence, Rhode Island
1969–86

Contents

1

Waltham

ॐ

I am a native of the Commonwealth of Massachusetts and of the city of Waltham, ten miles from Boston and its gold-topped state-house. I was born on the Fourth of July, 1899. The year I am happy about because it symbolically attached me to the nineteenth century which, in the United States as well as in England, continued until the First World War. Unlike my juniors, I can remember a period which, for middle-class people, was tranquil and steady. The day, however, was inappropriate and unfortunate, for in those same years the American holiday was not only patriotic but robustiously and noisily so. My childhood birthdays were made miserable by sudden sharp noises of firecrackers exploding and torpedoes hurled on the sidewalk just behind me by other boys who wanted the fun of seeing me jump.

Credible legend has it that my birth occurred during Waltham's Fourth of July parade. The day was properly hot. My mother, approaching the fullness of time, was sitting on the porch of the Warren house at 23 Prospect Street, when suddenly she felt a little uncomfortable. She was rushed upstairs; relaxed, she easily gave birth. I was named Edward Austin Warren Jr.

My mother's habitual state was relaxed—relaxed and dependent. She had a strong mother and a strong older sister. A pretty, dark-haired young woman, she fell in love with my father, a year her senior and a neighbor. They and their high school friends shared picnics and sleigh rides. My father had always the use of a carryall and a buggy and a good swift horse. He courted; he won; when he was twenty-one, he married her.

She had no wish for independence, even for a life of her own:

she existed to be loved and looked after: to be loved rather than to love, though in the passive she loved my father, and only him. She had no special desire for children; but they came—and to the then requisite Protestant number of two. I was born toward the end of the first year of marriage; my brother Russell, a year later.

My father, the only child of his parents to survive infancy, was a stout, blond, nearsighted—and already in childhood spectacled—boy, quick spirited, unambitious. His nearsightedness prevented him from becoming a sportsman, a player either of baseball or tennis; but it did not make him into a reader of books. And, though city reared, he disliked cities. As a boy, he used to drive up into the country with the men who went to collect the milk for his father's milk business: he was interested not in the delivery to the homes of Waltham customers but by the farms, the cows, the country.

When he was twenty-one, and ready to marry, my grandfather Warren built a small house for him, next door to the family home, and retired from his business, turning it over to his son. But upon my grandfather's death, my father sold the milk business and bought a farm at Ashburnham, in northeastern Massachusetts, almost at the New Hampshire line, a hilly village which he already knew as the summer home of the Goves, my grandmother's family. I dimly remember the white house with its brick ends, and lilac growing lavishly against the brick, where we lived for two years. My mother felt the isolation of the farm, missed her sisters and her school friends, and, for her sake, my father took the family back to Waltham.

For the next five years he owned and operated a double food shop on lower Main Street—one side of it a grocery, the other side, a market. He was an expert buyer of meat and an expert butcher. Thanks to the quality of his meat, his own transparent honesty, and his friendly and courteous manners, my father established a large carriage trade, and had the patronage of the wealthy Bostonians who had summer estates in the still extensive rural areas of Waltham. These fine folk, however, bought only on credit; and many gentlemen refused to pay except once a year, as they were about to move back to Boston for the winter, while some proved unwilling or unable to pay at all. In less than five years, the unpaid accounts had so mounted up that my father was forced to put them into the hands of a professional collector and to sell out. Something more was collected that way, but two or three thousand, a large sum for a small business, proved uncollectible. Neither then nor subsequently was my father a success at handling money—in this, quite unlike his father and his mother. It is my strong impression that from time to time my grandmother came to his financial rescue; and he was certainly never beyond financial worry till, after her death, he inherited her estate. Until then, he recurrently warned his family that we were about to "go to the poorhouse"—a Yankee enough foreboding.

Though not a success as a moneymaker, or perhaps partly because of this amiable weakness, my father was widely liked and respected in Waltham. Of the respect, the chief evidence is the fact that, though an entirely unpolitical man, he was urged to run as city alderman, was elected, and served till we left Waltham. His popularity was shown by the frequency by which he, a Protestant and a Republican, was invited to Irish wakes.

He had of course not lost his desire for the country. Soon after our return to Waltham, he built a simple two-story summer cottage at Ashburnham; in this cottage my mother and Russell and I spent July and August and my father his two weeks' vacation and his weekends, presumably then limited to Sundays. And when his business failed, my father's thoughts naturally turned back to farming. He had done his best, for my mother's sake, to endure city life; and he had not been able to succeed at it. My mother must again have been reluctant to leave Waltham; but this time my father's happiness was paramount to her, and the new move was not to so distant a place as Ashburnham, but to Stow, not more than twenty miles from Waltham.

The country farm was surely the right place for him, since he was not, like the city man, a specialist. He used to look down on his fellow Walthamites, who worked in the watch factory, who could do but one thing—who, when the factory shut down during a depression, had nothing else to which they could turn. How amused he was when these helpless men thought, upon their retirement, that they could run a chicken farm as a profit-making hobby. He had all the scorn of a Renaissance man or a frontiersman for these specialists, he who could do anything and repair anything—who could milk cows, build a load of hay, cut ice on the pond, or make apple boxes during the winter, who could mend a rake or sharpen a scythe; could slaughter his own cow, broil a steak, or tend an invalid. The small New England farm, subsistence farming—this was the last retreat of the archaic individualist, the autonomous man.

As is natural and appropriate, my father had no real use for scholars or clergymen or orators or any other men who lived by their skill with words—wordmongers and word hoarders and word manipulators. By his archaic standards, indeed, he really ruled out a good part of the human race. Even for businessmen, he had but limited respect, a part of the reason why, though skillful as a buyer of meat and a butcher, he failed at his market, and was so inept at accounts and at the collecting of bills. Anything savoring of commerce which was more abstract than trading a horse or a cow with a neighbor was really repugnant to him. He probably respected bankers like my "uncle" (we children were taught to call all older distant relatives Uncle or Aunt) Rob Gove more than professional men, especially the clergymen (whom he viewed, with some justification, from his early experiences of his mother's favorites, as the parasites of pious women); but he thought of traffic in figures—a paper transaction—as not much more honorable than traffic with words.

Of my mother, my memories are dim, especially of her in the Waltham years. She was good-humored, easygoing, much liked by her women friends whom she had acquired in high school. Neither then nor later was she much of a cook or a housekeeper. Nor was she much interested in either the theory or the practice of child rearing. Not on principle, but by temperament, she was a permissive mother. I cannot remember being punished, either by a spanking or by being denied my supper or by confinement to a closet or to my room. Nor was I taught table manners or any other kind of manners, or taught to hang up and look after my clothes, or any of the other elementary civilized routines. There were occasional injunctions to "wear my rubbers" or the like; but they were casual, intermittent, unsystematic, not followed up.

I never felt actively loved by my mother or needed by her, except as an ally when my father, moody in earlier years, had one of his frightening outbursts of temper. Indeed my brother and I were not "loved" children; rather, we were irrelevant. My parents were sufficient each to the other.

Our house, at 23 Prospect Street, was distinguished by the comparative grandeur of a corner lot; both the parlor and the sitting room behind it had bay windows; on the other side of the house was a dining room, shaded by two horse chestnut trees. Across the street stood a firehouse surmounted by a wooden campanile, from which, at nine each night, there sounded a curfew bell.

Beside the house was the only large yard in the neighborhood, behind it, a stable, which had once housed my grandfather's horse. This choice yard of ours was the natural playground for the neighborhood children. In the spring, we played store, setting up boxes as counters and dispensing lemonade and cookies to men and women walking by on their way to the watch factory. During the winter there were snow igloos and tunnels as well as snowmen and snowwomen. But mostly I remember, as from spring and fall, the game of cowboys and Indians—not, however, a game which I particularly enjoyed, for it was my inevitable role to play the captive, tied to a tree. From sports, games, I was excluded, for I never could learn, then or later, either to throw a ball or to catch one—could do no more than try, often unsuccessfully, not to be hit.

My brother Russell and I were classic opposites—Esau and Jacob, the extrovert and the introvert. He was the boy who played ball and in his teens owned a motorcycle and who, like our father, could make and fix things; and I was the boy who read books and picked out tunes on the piano, who liked church and school and who, when not reading, was daydreaming. We were, in some way, proud of each other; but, neither in childhood or later, had we many common interests or shared language. Only during his rare periods of illness would my brother let me show the affection I felt for him. He would normally have nothing to do with me—was embarrassed, certainly, by my complete failure to hold my own in the games which went on in our yard. Yet, loyal to his family, as he was and ever remained, he would come to my aid when things went too hard against me—when I was positively assaulted or laid low by the other boys.

I had another protector in Catharine McGuiness, the more or less tomboy who lived, with her parents and her four brothers and sisters, in an adjoining double house. These five Irish children whose father was a motorman on the trolley cars, were—the middle three of them—our contemporaries and chief playmates. Catharine was my loyal henchwoman and allowed no one either to attack or to tease me without a counterattack, often physical, from her; and she let me arrogantly dominate her—up to a point. I felt myself her superior because she was a girl and Irish and Catholic, because she did not live in a single house, and because her family owned no piano.

We had one powerful interest in common—religion; and about that we argued persistently and vigorously. I used to tell her that Catholics were forbidden by their priests to read the Bible, and remained unconvinced when she pointed to the big copy of the Douay Version which, undisturbed, lay on the parlor table. I denounced the statues Catholics idolatrously worshiped and their practice of confession of sins to priests instead of to God. Despite her personal devotion to me, Catharine remained unconverted to my ideas. After going through parochial school and high school and working as a stenographer for a year or two, she entered a convent and became a nun, saying to her mother, in strange, memorable words for such a girl to use, "I have tasted the pleasures of this world and never found them but vanity."

My boyhood antipathy against Catholicism—a mixture of horror and fear—was intense. St. Mary's, then the only Catholic church in Waltham, stood next door to our grammar school; and it fascinated me by its venerable red brick and ivy and stained glass, but I dared not enter its portal lest a priest seize me and lock me into a cell till I submitted to conversion. Such—and perhaps the guns stored in the basement for use when the time came to kill all Protestants—were the stories I had somehow heard, when or from whom I cannot guess. So strong was my boyhood Protestantism that when one of my schoolfellows, an Episcopalian who sang in the boy's choir at "low" Christ Church on Main Street, wanted me to join the choir, I, who knew that the Episcopal church was "next door to the Catholic," firmly declined.

Like most literary folk, I cannot remember when I could not read, though my recollections of what I read scarcely go back of the age of ten. I was then a collector of Horatio Alger's books about poor city boys who vanquished bullies (as I could not) and were conscientious in returning to stout old gentlemen their carelessly dropped money or their gold watches—figures nearer to my urban and Yankee mind than the books about the Motor Boat Boys and Submarine Boys, young heroes of the out-of-doors and sports, which gave pleasure to my brother Russell.

One summer in Ashburnham, when I was eleven or twelve, I drew from the public library Howard Pyle's *Otto of the Silver Hand*, a story about the young son of a medieval robber baron who was caught by a rival robber baron and deprived of a hand. His father, recapturing him and giving him a substitute hand of silver, decided that a mountain fortress was no suitable home for a frail and bookish boy and handed him over to white-robed monks to rear. This narrative, and Mrs. Mulocks's *Little Lame Prince*, with its fragile hero who was given in compensation for his handicap a pair of magical spectacles and a corresponding pair of magical eardrums, extending his sight and his hearing far beyond those of other boys, gave me the nearest boy-figures with which I could identify—I, who, though neither lame nor lacking a hand, nor even shortsighted, was physically ineffectual, and a daydreamer. Mostly, I had to resort to books by women written primarily for girls— especially the English books of a generation back: Mrs. Mole-worth's *The Cuckoo Clock*, with its tale of an imaginative little girl alone in an old house with her great-aunts, was a particular favorite.

Of the literary genres, the fairy tale most attracted me. I was given, almost upon its appearance, L. Frank Baum's *The Wizard of Oz* with its illustrations by W. W. Denslow; and this book, though it grew battered and dog-eared, I held on to till, in middle life, I felt again unembarrassedly free to read fairy tales. Other favorites were Joseph Jacobs's *English Fairy Tales* and Andrew Lang's *Red Fairy Book*, especially the latter. But the Oz books were the most precious. When Christmas came, Aunt Etta's gift, ever the newest book in the series, was the one I most eagerly opened, after which came the other packages which were book shaped. I was much disappointed if my parents gave me, as they often did, some "useful" present like underwear—things with which I would have to be provided any way. And I found it hard to be duly grateful for the single silver teaspoon, with my name engraved on it, which annually was the gift of my great-grand-mother Butler. Books were what I wanted; and, I was proud when, at ten or twelve, I found the number of Christmas books mounting to perhaps a dozen.

These gifts I could later supplement by my own purchases. My grandmother Dillingham gave both my brother and me a small allowance, fifteen or twenty-five cents a week, expressly that we might learn the value of saving, and prudently spending, money. Mine naturally went for books. In those days Everyman's Library sold at thirty-five cents a copy; and it gave me intense pleasure, when my grandmother took me with her on a trip to Boston, to go into a book shop and buy a Waverly novel in red and gold, the binding Everyman's then wore. Scott was the first of the "classical" novelists to interest me; and I acquired about ten of his novels, of which my favorite was *Redgauntlet*, before I shifted to buying Dickens in the same edition.

My father took in partial payment for a grocery bill a golden oak card catalogue; and, proudly, I turned my room, the hall bed-room on top of the stairs, into a "public library," made out library cards for all my books, and issued loans to my friends. At this time, as I remember, I thought of growing up to become a librarian, in the innocent assumption that I then could spend my days reading.

I began, too, to write—which gave me added and more ambitious thought of authorship. The division of a novel into chapters having deeply impressed me, I began my own creative work by dividing a composition book into chapters, each four pages long, and each provided with a title—after which I fitted my story into the framework. Some of the narratives were modeled on Horatio Alger, and some apparently on Walter Scott, for I remember *The Cross and the Crescent* as the title of one. But the effort of which I was most proud was a tale about a brownie. For it, my pretty Sunday school teacher, Miss Stevens, made me three illustrations in watercolor, and I myself bound it, as I did also some miniature anthologies of quotations from Longfellow and Whittier, the household poets whom we were made to memorize at school.

My public and formal education began at five. I was briefly enrolled in the Banks School, scarcely a block away from our house, and was there taught by the same venerable Miss Peabody who had taught my father when he began school. Having spent her life teaching the very young, Miss Peabody spoke in the voice of a little child. Then I have a brief memory of a one- or two-room country schoolhouse at Ashburnham, and after that nothing before the eighth and ninth grades in the Waltham Grammar School, over which Mr. Bradford Drake, my first male teacher, presided as principal with Yankee dignity and shrewdness.

I have no recollection of having disliked school or of having felt myself too bright for it. I was apparently neither bored nor excited by the instruction; was docile in the presence of my elders and not persecuted by my contemporaries. But I did not awaken, did not look up (as about the same age I began to do at the sermon in church) till I reached the classes of Miss Childs, a white-haired woman who taught me English grammar in the eighth grade and Latin grammar in the ninth. Waltham was a pioneer in beginning the study of a foreign language before high school.

The formal structure of grammar—and in those days English grammar was taught after the paradigm of Latin—was my introduction to classification and logic, to "thought"; and I responded. I responded eagerly, too, to Latin and the many ways in which Latin etymologies lit up the meaning of English words I was using. I had long loved words and collected them as other boys collected marbles or the pictures of baseball players which used then to come in packages of cigarettes. Now, in Latin, I possessed a magic control over my English words; and I began, so far as I could, to talk like a dictionary.

This new interest in language as a system led to my buying a book on Esperanto, a language which, with the aid of my Latin, I did not find difficult to learn. I organized the Waltham Esperanto Society, and made myself president of a small group of friends.

The word *friends* comes from my pen with joy. Until my last two years in grammar school, while Russell had many companions, I had none save loyal Catharine, a girl. But then I made two real friendships with boys of bookish interest who lived each only a block away and were in my grade at school—Carl Ellis and Irving Garfield. There were, I then found, other boys who liked words and books and studies! I was no longer alone, an alien and a misfit. Perhaps it was part of this newfound assurance that I learned to swim and bicycle, two forms of physical activity which are relatively uncompetitive. Yet these were my last male friends of my own age, temperament, and concerns till I reached college.

Sunday was my favorite day, for in the morning there was church, and in the afternoon there was a visit to my mother's elder sister, Aunt Etta, the only real lover of reading I knew and the only storyteller.

I was religiously educated at the First Methodist Church of Waltham. The minister who received me into the church—at eleven or twelve—was the Reverend James E. Coons, a westerner from Ohio or Kansas or Nebraska (New Englanders couldn't differentiate those distant states). My brother and I were taken to church more or less regularly by our mother. Sensibly, we were allowed to carry storybooks with us to read during that adult part of "church," the sermon. But, during my last years at Waltham, beginning to have an appetite for ideas, I looked up more and more frequently from my book to listen to the preacher. I no longer needed my fairy tale.

For me, as a child, religion was primarily a social and aesthetic ritual, differentiating caste from caste and school days from Sunday. From the first, I had pleasure in the tone and mood of religion—which was solemn and beautiful. I liked dressing up; I liked the sound of the organ, and I liked ritual. I first apprehended church as a kind of society in which people try to look their best and to behave at their best, or at their conception of their best. As a child, I took in, without knowing what or where God is, that people were presenting themselves to be inspected—or endorsed or comforted—by the best they knew to exist. Religion was a social and emotional dedication to some invisible and not really articulable cause: that I perceived.

As long as we lived in Waltham, Aunt Etta allotted each Sunday afternoon to Russell and me. She read aloud to us—sometimes from Kipling's *Just-So Stories* or *Jungle Book*, sometimes from *Uncle Remus* or the stories of Frank R. Stockton or Miss Wilkins (a favorite of hers as, later, of mine). But even better, we relished, and demanded, the stories she made up for us. She had created a world of Cabbage Fairies; and, though she herself wearied of this cycle, and would have preferred sometimes to tell us an unrelated story, we would allow her no exception.

The pleasure with which I remember my aunt's improvised tales speaks negatively for the absence of other storytellers or storytelling in the family—the difference between the Yankee world of my boyhood and the world of my southern literary contemporaries with their vast family sagas, told ever with leisurely embellishments. What Warren, Gove, Anderson, and Myrick matter I could extract from my elders was scant; the anecdotes were undeveloped.

Aunt Etta lived close to us, in Waltham, with her mother, Grandma Anderson (the Andersons, my mother's family, were of Scotch extraction; my grandmother, born a Myrick, of Welsh). Grandma Anderson competed, never successfully but never surrendering, with my formidable grandmother Warren, later Mrs. Isaac Snow Dillingham of Auburndale. These two women were of different religions and differently equipped, propertywise, and of different temperaments, so that from boyhood on I had two types of life and two worlds, each self-coherent, to observe and study.

Grandma Anderson was the hedonist, the conservative, and the skeptic; Grandma Dillingham (called by us children "Ma," as our father had called her; she never seemed old or infirm enough to be called Grandma) was the believer and doer.

Grandma Anderson was a professional invalid who lived to be over ninety. She took to her bed when she was thirty-five; and thereafter, little as her husband could afford it, she kept a servant—till the time came when the Irish women had graduated from being maids and the Scandinavians, their successors, had also graduated. The evil day arrived about 1920; and the Andersons then had to engage a housekeeper, someone who sat with the family at meals and in the sitting room, if she had a mind to.

What Grandma Anderson lived by was not easy to make out. She was not a religious woman, even in old age. Reared a Congregationalist, she may have sat, as a girl, under some theologically minded, ancient Calvinist; but, if so, it had made no doctrinal impression upon her. She regarded all active forms of religion as so many forms of bad taste, and used to make me wince with her satire of the Warren Methodism. In her girlhood, she lived near a camp meeting, and she recalled its shoutings and convulsions and hearty hymn-singing. She was probably well aware that the old-time Methodism had disappeared, but she had no wish to admit it. Methodism was eccentric and sentimental—therefore disorderly and comic; and that was the end of the matter.

Herself, she was skeptically conservative. Changes of religion had about them something indecent as well as humorless. As from changing from the religion one was reared in, that was taking the whole business with a seriousness unwarranted. After all, we don't really know anything about the beyond and the hereafter; hence well-bred people have always stayed by the religion in which they were reared. She did not pray or read the Bible, at least in her last years; and to me she expressed, undisturbed but mildly speculative, her doubts concerning the future life. Yet these insolubles didn't interest her. She did not develop her doubts or speculations. Thin and narrow, Grandma was neither bitter nor confused. Her central view of life was dryly satiric.

Yet when her claims of invalidism had been accepted, and, accepted, released her from her work, entitling her, for the rest of her life, to the easiest chair and the first look at the evening newspaper, she had energy enough to play—till, bored, she "went upstairs"—the role of a detached, ironic, even whimsical observer of life.

Louise Gove, successively Mrs. Warren and Mrs. Dillingham, was the dominant member of the Warren family. A lady, of some means and some social position, she could have used, intelligently, real wealth and adorned almost any station. Like so many masterful Victorians, English and American, she was compounded of contraries which, though never integrated, held up, and together, through a lifetime. She could generally win what she wanted by strength of will or intellectual clarity; but, on occasions when these powers seemed inadequate, she could turn to the feminine repertory of cajolery and tenderness.

She had marked gifts as an administrator and organizer, and had a clear head for business. She was the inevitable president of any group to which she belonged; and, by her judicious buying and selling of stocks and bonds, she not only preserved, but substantially increased, what she had inherited from her father, Austin Gove, the coal merchant of East Boston, and from her first husband, George Edward Warren, the milk dealer. Of my grandmother, as of another "elect lady," it might have been said that she read two books faithfully every day—her Bible and her stock market reports. She practiced the counsel of John Wesley: "Make all you can; save all you can; give all you can." But she did not believe in confounding these successive precepts: did not, that is, believe in mixing charity with business. She exacted the full value of their wages from her servants, who nonetheless respected her, since she asked them to do nothing at which she was not herself adept.

Her education was completed at Bradford Academy, just across the river from Haverhill. In her day, Bradford was a finishing school, offering, in addition to French and other refined studies, rigorous training in deportment. Even in her old age, my grandmother maintained her fine carriage as she walked; and, when she sat, it was with a dignified and impressive erectness which made a straight-backed chair the most comfortable. Her posture she attributed to the regimen of the academy, which prescribed backboards to habituate the students to erectness. At Bradford, she made intimate friends, two of whom, women of character and bearing, I long after met. The years at Bradford must have given her character the aristocratic tone which differentiated her from her Methodist associates.

My grandmother, two years after her husband's death, married a widower, Isaac Snow Dillingham, upwards of ten years her senior, a handsome man, like herself a Methodist (Grandfather Warren had been reared a New England Unitarian). Mr. Dillingham had, before the Boston fire of 1870, been a wealthy man; then had been a bankrupt; now operated a one-man cotton brokerage in Boston; had an invalid first wife of luxurious tastes and three children; lived beyond his means. My grandmother paid off his debts; refurbished his house in Auburndale, one of the Newtons, "refined" suburbs of Boston; made him a most congenial wife, mother to his ungrown youngest daughter, and hostess.

My father, who resembled his milk-dealer father, disapproved of his new stepfather as a "four-flusher." I, who did not remember my grandfather, was fond of Mr. Dillingham and his style and way of life, the grandest I knew. I was often, as boy and youth, a guest in the household; I admired its ostensible head, and his home, and Auburndale, a marked social contrast to Waltham, as my new grandfather, something of a tease, never ceased to remind me.

The Dillingham house, on Woodland Road, in Auburndale, stood opposite the Congregational church, whose bell struck deep, mellow hours. The house appeared set in rather spacious grounds. Though they did not really belong to Grandpa, vacant lots adjoined the house on both sides; so that the property mastered a block; and the sense of "grounds" was helped out by flowering shrubs—dogwood and syringas—left and right of the path up to the house.

The arrangement of the Dillingham house conformed, apparently, to the mode of Auburndale, which was the mode of Boston. The family lived on the second floor, descending only for the solemn meals in the dining room. Indeed, the ground floor was rarely used. A wide hall led from the central front door to the stairs at the further end; and, even from the entrance, one could see a full-length mirror, baroquely framed in gold, which backed, a few shallow steps up, the first landing of the stair. The floor of the hall was carpeted tightly, up to the baseboards, with red velvet. From either side of the hall opened parlors. The left-hand room, in front of the dining room, had been fitted up, at her own expense, by the second Mrs. Dillingham. Termed the Reception Room, it was used for callers who should not be made too comfortable lest they stay too long. The room was neat, crisp, immaculate, but uninteresting: an American rug of undistinguished design, a modern mahogany table, a window seat with cushions of green plush, a black walnut bookcase.

The other side of the hall was given to a double parlor—never used, because never refurbished—an unacknowledged remainder from the first Mrs. Dillingham. Portieres shut these rooms off from the hall, and the draperies were generally drawn. Within, the upholstery was damask—faded, and, in the back parlor, tattered. The two parlors were separated by a central chimney, allowing a small but ornate fireplace to open on to each of them. There was a black upright piano, its case decorated by panels of cutwork; beside it stood an ornate black cabinet with open shelves gathering dust upon sheet music and music albums. The parlors had a faded and muffled grandeur more to my taste than my grandmother's Reception Room.

Only special intimates of the family were invited to come upstairs, where, like other Auburndale women, my grandmother had her sitting room. A couch in red stood in the bay window; before it, an elegant little walnut writing desk. At this desk, my grandmother wrote letters in her clear, firm, Spencerian hand, carried on her transactions in stocks and bonds, wrote checks, and added up her monthly bank statement. Into this room came Mrs. Professor Bates, lean, pince-nezed, black-ribboned of neck, and Mrs. Sophronia Butters, wife of "dear Dr. Butters," pastor of Centenary Methodist Church, and also her old friends from Bradford Academy.

In that upstairs sitting room, the Dillinghams knelt on the carpet for family prayers, my grandfather almost as eloquent as he was at church in the Friday night prayer meeting. And there, after our early evening meal in the dining room (snowy linen cloth under Tiffany suspended shade, well-trained cook serving), the Dillinghams read aloud to each other, and their boy guest, generally from Dickens.

Between Waltham and Auburndale, I, always between worlds, was torn; and I early learned to play their claims against each other and to mediate between them. On the whole, and obviously, I preferred the world of the Dillinghams. It was a world of dignity and at least seeming stability, the upper-middle-class world of the Victorians. It was a class-conscious world: but that class consciousness was not one merely of money but of standards of living and social behavior and social responsibility. And it did not doubt the justice of its own worldviews.

In another, and important, sense, both sets of grandparents stood together in my mind as against my parents and their generation; and here I was clearly on the side of my grandparents. I see now, it was that older generation to which I looked for standards, for something firm and fixed upon which to pattern myself, by which I might measure myself. My parents and their friends seemed by comparison weak and ineffectual, without beliefs of their own—their religion and their politics taken on trust from their parents—their rebellion no more than a dilution of what they had inherited.

The cultural life of Waltham was represented in my grandmother Warren's time by a Theosophical Society founded after a visit from Swami Vivekananda, and the Browning-Emerson Club, of which my grandmother was a regular, if somewhat puzzled, member. Later on, cultural life took form in a Shakespeare Club and an active musical society, of which our neighbors, Mrs. Barker, and my cousin Walter Starbuck were luminaries. And Waltham had its own excellent newspaper, the *Free-Press Tribune*, edited by Walter's father, Alexander Starbuck, a witty and scholarly man whose history of his ancestral Nantucket is still standard.

It was chiefly a misfortune, I think, that, at thirteen just as I was emerging from haze and reverie and approaching something like consciousness, I had to be transplanted, and to a country village. Waltham, in the years before the first war, was less a suburb than a relatively autonomous New England city—with its own cultural community, and yet within an hour's ride by streetcar or half an hour by railroad, from Boston. And Auburndale was but three miles away, to support my standards and aspirations and ambitions.

2

Stow

ಎ

The social structure of Stow, ten miles north of Emerson's Concord, was that of rural New England—at first sight, classless; the
ordinary life of the village, Protestant Yankee. The village was
divided into pious Evangelicals who attended our church, the
Union Church, and did not dance, play cards, or go to the theater,
and the worldly and sinful Unitarians who did all three. The Unitarians occupied the old white meetinghouse which stood in the
common; unquestionably, they had a slight social precedence over
the Evangelicals—such as they then, at least, still had in almost
every New England village within easy distance from Harvard College. There was an air of worldliness about them, as of people who
went to Boston from time to time and perhaps visited the Parker
House or some other hotel where liquor was served. Few worshipers attended the services of the First Parish Church, presided
over by the elderly and strange bachelor, the Reverend J. Sidney
Moulton; but the Fletchers and the Derbys contributed to their
suppers and bazaars, and their children sang in the Unitarian choir.

The Warren farm was a mile from the village. The rambling,
thirteen-roomed house admitted of subdivision and segregation.
The front parlor and the parlor bedroom over it could not be heated
by the furnace and were shut off from the rest of the house.
Though smallish as well as square, both rooms had white wain-
scoting and an air of dignity.

The parlor was my precinct and domain; for it held the walnut
piano, beside which stood the oil stove, meagerly heating the room
when, in the depth of winter, I undertook my daily practice. I also
retreated to the privacy of this room whenever my temper got the

17

better of me. I was often in a fury over something my parents had said, which crossed my will or vanity; and on these occasions— since it was unchristian to explode—I took out my rage on the piano, in loud and violent extemporization.

A stairway to the back bedrooms opened between the sitting room and the library, and at the top of it were three rooms. My brother Russell and I slept in a narrow room over the kitchen, a room with slanting roof reached through a passageway—a low, arched ceiling and wooden walls lined with cupboards for the storing of linens. Since we both read, after undressing, and often went to sleep over our books, our father rigged up a long cord which went from our room to his bed and allowed him to pull out our light without leaving the warmth of the bedclothes. In preparation for going to bed on a winter night all of the family were provided with soapstones drawn from the oven of the kitchen range and wrapped in cloth.

Behind the large kitchen stretched a long summer kitchen; and behind that was the butler's pantry, used for the storage of provisions. Throughout the winter, it held meats hanging from the ceiling or the wall—shoulders of beef and ham, perhaps a whole pig, extracted from the supply of pigs which lived in the barn cellar, and half a dozen hens from the coops in the back of the barn. In the summer, generally with the aid of "Ma" Whitcom, an elderly neighbor, my mother put up all sorts of preserves: peaches and pears, strawberries, raspberries, plums; conserves of various kinds; mustard pickles in brine, from our own always abundant cucumbers, piccalilli and chili sauce for use on the ever-present baked beans; then all sorts of jellies, each put into its little jar with melted wax over it.

The barn was larger and higher than the house—a cathedral of a barn, I used to think. A long lintel for the cows ran down one side; on the other were stalls for the horses, with adjoining rooms wardrobed with rich leather harnesses. Over each aisle was a great haymow, full to overflowing at the end of the summer, when the second crop had been garnered, and empty as spring approached. My fancy wanted to put a reed organ in the empty hay galleries, both to carry out the ecclesiastical structure of the well-made barn and also, upon a hint from the *Etude*, my monthly musical magazine, to aid the rhythm of the milking. The art of milking I never learned. The reason given by my father to the neighbors was that to milk would stiffen my fingers for the playing of the piano; that

I was not going to be a farmer. But I had my repugnances as well; I felt the operation indecently physical.

Horses, which I learned to harness and to drive, after a fashion, were splendid creatures, even though all "gift horses" retired from the Waltham Fire Department. Splendid but terrifying, they moved regally and rapidly on their iron-shod hoofs. They challenged one who liked breaking another's will, or proving one's mastery of the intractable. But I was not instinctively roused to competition or by danger; and I was afraid of the horses, of which naturally they were aware.

The cows were my favorite animals. They were mystics and philosophers, pursuing their ruminations rhythmically—undisturbed, unperturbed by accident of time and space, of flies and dung. Creatures of large general benevolence, they seemed incapable, after weaning the annual calf, of private attachments or hostilities.

During perhaps five months of the year the cows were turned out to pasture, even as late as September, when the grass had already been closely cropped; for the farmer's intent was twofold: to provide them food and to give them exercise and freedom to lie, to stroll, to bathe in brook or pool.

Our pasture, which lay across the road from the house and barn, extended to fifty acres. To convoy the cows across the high road and into the lane was never anything but difficult, and required the services of our whole family. In transit, the cows were, as the old hymn says, "prone to wander," to meditate in the middle of the road, to climb over the wall into the September orchard, there to eat fallen apples till they became reelingly drunk and their milk became too sour to market.

In those early days, there were few automobiles; but, especially in the afternoon when they were returning to the barn, the cows were likely to encounter pedestrians or a horse and buggy; and then, with the indecision of Coleridge, they could not determine whether to move left or right: they had no thought-out course of action, but stood till they obstructed all passage, and then moved with such panicky rapidity as to kick the farmer or step on a stray hen.

Papa, Mama, Russell, and I used all to station ourselves at the corners of an imagined square or oblong to enclose and steer the animals; but a cow often eluded one of her guards and went careening up the road, with two or three of us in heated pursuit. Then

Papa would lose his temper; Mama begin to cry with nervous vexation; and I who shared the cows' uncertainty which course to take, would be uncomfortably apprehensive that I would fail my father in this crisis.

Four o'clock was the time for me to "go after the cows." In midsummer, this duty meant release from tedding, raking, or apple picking—at none of which I was competent. I started out alone up the lane, which, gently ascending, reached at its other end a mile away the top of a hill, from which one could see, spread out before him, the steeples of two or three villages. Generally the cows, lying down, awaited me at the top of the hill. The walk up was reverie in the warm, sleepy, mellow sunlight of late afternoon. I held a stick in my hand, a light branch lopped off from some birch; on the way, I stopped to pick a few wild strawberries growing by the path or some checkerberry leaves, glossy, dark green to the sight and palatable to chew. Halfway to the hill, I passed the blueberry swamp, where, on many hot afternoons, my brother Russell and I filled tinkling milk pails with berries extracted from the high bushes, picking with one hand while with the other we waved away flies and mosquitoes.

The way up was happy. Never botanical nor ornithological, I could name little that I saw, but yielded myself, passively and pantheistically, to the perfect whole, experiencing Nature rather than objects. I felt, of the trees and flowers as of the cows, that I did not want to know their "hinder parts." I preferred prospects to immediacies, the vague to the precise. I looked over Jordan to "Canaan's fair and happy land." But I was a sensuous as well as—by the time of adolescence—a mystical boy and I had intense though diffuse pleasure in the vaguer senses of touch, taste, and odor, and especially body feeling. It was the total embrace—of air, wind, sun, or rain—to which I surrendered.

On our own land, slanting down from the summit, lay a sparse woodland of deciduous trees called, by some visitor, the "Italian garden," by virtue of its Lombardy poplars or some New England equivalents. The "garden" intimated a Europe unseen; I used to fancy that one day I would build a house in the garden. Those few minutes at the top of the hill constituted the climax of my day. There I felt at one with an immanent Presence; it was a quiet joy.

Going after the cows, with its mild trance at the hilltop was my chief summer pleasure, the more so as I was also helping my father, was being of use. I was of less use in other forms of summer work—with the haying, for example; for, though the tractors had not yet superseded the horse, machines of other sorts were already used, and I, belatedly medieval and primitive of mind, feared machines, which, unlike men and animals, could not be talked to or reasoned with, or reached by feeling.

I dutifully mowed, raked, and tedded; but my fear of machines, added to my fear of horses, and the hilly nature of the orchards in which I was told to work, rendered me ineffectual. Once I fell off the seat of the tedder and into the curved prongs intended to gather the grass into winnows. Seeing what had happened, my father was alarmed; but I was rescued unbruised and but dimly conscious of what had happened. It was my father's notion that the accident had occurred because I was "thinking of books": he might as well have said, "thinking of God." Neither diagnosis was accurate, but I thought to myself that either would serve to rescue me from the tendance of machines.

My father could manage both animals and machines; he was one of the first to buy a Ford; and my younger brother Russell was licensed to drive at the earliest legal age. Both my father and my brother were adept to work with machines and tools. If, as was often the case in early years, a tire was punctured, they could jack up the car, remove the wheel, and install the spare—all without anxiety. They could deal expertly with a troubled motor or carburetor. They understood the visibly elaborate structure of an automobile.

With two such experts always at hand, neither my mother or I ever learned to drive a car. That we should do so was never suggested to us; and we were too aware of our mechanical incompetence to request instructions not offered.

In the winter, after coming home from high school, Russell and I both had our chores to do. Russell helped my father with the milking. I, too, had some barn chores: feeding the cows and, when we had them, the hens, are what I recall; these were routine chores which I performed faithfully, even ritualistically, and with a dependability for which my father praised me. But my chief chores, which followed, were inside the house, in the assistance of my mother. I helped to set the supper table and with the washing and wiping of the dishes. In the summer time, I shelled the peas; in the winter, I ground the meat and potatoes for one of our staple and favorite foods, corned beef hash. My chief household activity was cooking, however, and more particularly baking.

My mother never made yeast bread—what country folk called "riz bread"; but, like other farm and generally American households, our family liked and frequently had all kinds of hot, quickly made breads—graham and corn muffins, popovers and baking powder biscuits; and for Saturday night supper we had New England steamed brown bread, served with our home-baked beans, and reheated for breakfast on Sunday.

All these hot breads I used to manufacture; but cakes were my specialty—whether white, or devil's food chocolate, or spice—customarily topped with chocolate frosting, which I mixed up in a yellow bowl. There were so few things I could do with my hands that, after playing the piano, baking took next place among my pleasures at artistry, at creative work.

What did my mother and I talk about as we worked together in the kitchen? Certainly not about the things which centrally mattered to me—which would be religion, music, and books. Our talk must have been a form of phatic communion—talk about the household operations we were jointly engaged in, or news from the village—the affairs of the church, the Grange, and the Civic Club—or about our relatives, including the rival grandmothers.

This was my world at home, a mile from the village, where the Warrens lived, a chiefly self-sufficient family. Outside it were the church and the high school. To the latter, Russell and I, equipped with lunch boxes containing deviled ham and peanut butter sandwiches and cake, journeyed forth in a buggy drawn by our old gray horse, "parked"in the Unitarian minister's horse shed till our return.

The Hale High School of Stow, in my time, never exceeded fifty students; and I had the good fortune to be there taught by three excellent teachers—the bachelor principal, Frederick J. Simmons, who was a graduate of the University of Maine, and two women, graduates respectively of Radcliffe and Wellesley. The smallness of the student body made possible a closer concern with individual students than a large high school like that of Waltham could have managed.

It precluded, but to no disadvantage, the wide and loose curriculum of progressive city schools. Latin was soundly, and indeed also affectionately, taught by the principal—a circumstance largely responsible, doubtless, for my classical major at college. It was not possible to include Greek as well, or French; but German, then occupying the primacy among modern languages, was so well taught that it became my second mastered language at Wesleyan.

Chemistry and physics were offered in alternate years. I

profited from neither. My experiments in the chemical laboratory often failed to turn out successfully; but, even when they did, I felt them to be not experiments but simply, at best, correct reproductions of what chemists in the past, in chemical history, had already worked out.

Mathematics was yet worse. I never got beyond algebra and plane geometry; but even these reduced me, by my failure to comprehend them, to tears. I did the only thing I could do: memorizing formulas. Yet seeing, later, that mathematics is a mode of philosophy, and dimly apprehending the justice of Plato's exclusion from his Academy of those geometrically ignorant, I could not but feel that I must have been improperly taught: had mathematics been philosophically presented, surely I would not only have been spared the embarrassment at my public tears but would have received an induction into abstract thinking.

How many subjects are taught, even by good teachers, as formula and rote, are taught neither from the teacher's interior apprehension or, philosophically, in terms of "first principles!" My English teacher, the Radcliffe graduate, a woman probably not over thirty, was utterly, painfully, New Englandly, conscientious; but she taught Shakespeare as though his plays were a discipline in parsing Elizabethan English and in learning Rolfe's notes. It was incredible that she had any feeling for poetry and that she liked Shakespeare, for she made me hate the Shakespeare she taught.

Indeed it was only when—under another and literary teacher, with whom I read Virgil, that I first "saw" and "heard" poetry. Unlike the other, this young woman was not a "schoolmistress." Though technically a spinster, she had, so it seemed to me, lived and loved; how else, indeed, could she understand literature? How else, indeed, could she not conscientiously hate or at least distrust it as libertine and inexact?

By the law of the Commonwealth of Massachusetts, the principal was required to open each school day with a reading from the Bible. To a conscientious agnostic, this was a case of conscience, narrowly restricting him to what he could read—almost to chapters from Job and Proverbs and Ecclesiastes, the last an agnostic work got into the canon by its pseudonymous ascription to Solomon and by the pious counterstatements incoherently inserted by rabbis. The principal's favorite was the third chapter of Ecclesiastes, which I would have found utterly depressing had it not been for the poetic parallelism which turned it into litany.

To every thing there is a season . . .
A time to be born, and a time to die:
a time to plant, and a time to pluck up that which is planted.

Classes apart, I continued to be isolated at school—even from
the reasonably well-bred and intelligent young who should, I felt,
have been my friends.

When I first entered the Stow High School, my contemporary,
Bill Sundberg, a strange mixture of the brilliant pupil and the
bully, quickly seized me up, and, in the basement lunchroom, on
no pretext, knocked me unconscious. My younger brother Russell
came to my rescue and knocked out Sundberg. That was the only
episode of the sort, but I could scarcely feel more gratitude than
embarrassment, since to be defended by my younger brother was
almost like being defended by my loyal girl cohort of Waltham,
Catharine.

The lunch hour I found ever awkward if not indeed positively
painful. All the other pupils ate at utmost speed, leaving at least a
half hour to the boys for ball and to the girls for chat. An outsider
and alien, excluded from both groups, and with no equally excluded friend to talk with, I desired only escape. In my senior year,
I used to take my lunch box and leave school for the duration of
the noon hour. I had found, at no more than a ten-minute walk, a
proper and solacing retreat: a scarcely used road with a graveyard
on one side and a gentle birch-shaded brook on the other.

The only way in which I could at all ingratiate myself with
my fellow pupils was by playing the piano for marching and dancing. Though it was sinful, of course, to true Christians, who must
keep themselves unspotted from the world, yet dancing (like card
playing, drinking, smoking, and theatergoing) was permissible to
Catholics on the one hand and to Unitarians on the other; and
my conscience assured me that I was not leading them astray.

The issue of worldly amusements was seriously raised when
the senior class went to Boston to see a play of Shakespeare's—
Hamlet or *Macbeth*. It was a "case of conscience" indeed for me.
Though I had acquired no taste for the dramatist, I knew that
Shakespeare was "culture."But Shakespeare wrote plays performed
in the theaters; and Christians knew that theaters were sinful. In
my dilemma, I sought the spiritual direction of my pastor. The
young Methodist, however, appeared unable to muster a dogmatic
answer; and I was left to my own conscience, which convinced

me that in the name of holiness I must abstain from this species of culture.

Though the Warren family was chiefly self-sufficient and self-enclosed, we were on good terms with our neighbors and the village generally. My father, all his life a good mixer, genial and upon occasion gregarious, rose to be first a selectman of Stow and later to be chairman of the selectmen. We did not lack suitable social life. My parents were members of the local Grange, the Patrons of Husbandry, originally a nonsecret order for farmers and their wives. Not old enough to join the Grange, my brother and I were both free to accompany our parents to the Civic Club, founded and presided over by Mr. Moulton, the elderly minister of the Unitarian church, an intellectual with intellectual friends in Boston. This club, which met monthly for a supper, included the chief members of both the rival churches. After the supper, lectures, sometimes illustrated by stereopticon slides, were given by the out-of-town speakers—lectures at once popular and instructive, a kind of continuation of the New England Lyceum.

The social occasions I most enjoyed were the suppers held in the basement of our Union church. This room, depressing when unused, was cheerful, even gay, when a supper was in progress. The churchwomen, most of the week segregated in their own kitchens, "visited" with each other as they served up their contributions. Every woman brought the dish for which she was locally celebrated—her baked beans or baked macaroni or boiled ham, her pickles, or her pumpkin pie. The food was abundant and hearty, and so were the talk and the laughter.

And after the supper, sometimes requiring several sittings, came a program of "home talent," including some recitations but chiefly music. My high school classmate, Dorothy Peck, and I were the rival piano soloists: she played Chopin or Schubert; I, MacDowell or Nevin. She performed with precision, I with much feeling, sentimentally. William Peck had a brief period of playing the silver cornet. And, in a powerful nasal tenor, Carl Thompson sang to my accompaniment.

My chief interests, solaces, and stays during my high school years were religion and music. The Union Evangelical Church of Stow—Methodists and Baptists, a union of Trinitarian Congregationalists, partly doubtless because it was a rural church—held to a much more conservative faith than that of Waltham, nearer to what was later called Fundamentalism. Such a doctrine was less what was preached—for our young pastors studied at the liberal Boston University School of Theology—than what the church members believed, and, believing supposed that they were hearing from the pulpit. Congregations are commonly more conservative, or superstitious, than their pastors. If the Protestant pastor continues, as he habitually did in those days, to use the customary terminology—the "blessed words," *salvation, redemption, incarnation,* and *grace,* the elderly church members assume him to mean by those words what the words mean to them. Both the young pastors who served the church during my high school years certainly believed in Evangelical religion as a pragmatic system, but certainly neither held the faith which was the common faith of their parishioners.

Though I listened with pleasure to their sermons, the instruments of propaganda and conditioning which did effectual work on me were the Sunday school, the Christian Endeavor Society, the Friday evening prayer meeting, and the devotional songs from the "red book." The Bible and the gospel hymns are the sacraments and ikons of Evangelical Protestantism. As a new member of the Christian Endeavor Society, I took my pledge to read a chapter of the Bible daily; and this I did faithfully throughout high school.

A deep influence on my high school self was Frank Sargent, a tall, ungainly half-wit, for a time the living-in hired man on our farm. Frank, a pious bachelor, who neither drank nor smoked, spent his spare time—at noon and at night, in the kitchen—reading his Bible and his weekly magazine, issued by the Moody Bible Institute of Chicago. It was he who awakened me to the menace of "Liberalism."Frank would get excited as he attacked those dangerous, unnamed figures called "the higher critics," who were "blasting at the Rock of Ages." Though you couldn't really damage or diminish the Rock—at least, not any more than farmers like my father could diminish the endless supply of ledge rock which underlay their land and which used periodically to be dynamited, it was nonetheless impious of those higher critics to try.

Out of my daily Bible reading, I drew special texts to be my inspiration and stay. My very special text was "I can do all things through Christ who strengtheneth me"—a mighty text for a besieged and isolated young Christian.

If the Bible was my chief book, Sunday was my favorite day. To inebriate me, there were four services at our church—morning preaching, Sunday school, Christian Endeavor at six-thirty, and evening services. The order was, for excitement, an ascending one.

The young people's meeting, to which I walked alone, came after my Sunday afternoon journey to the pasture; I sometimes led the meeting, and almost always "offered prayer" or "testified" or both; and I was chairman of the Missionary Committee—had, in short, the otherwise denied opportunities and delights of self-expression.

At the evening service, instead of using the church hymnal (more or less austere in its poetry and music) the congregation sang from the red book of gospel hymns. Most thrilling to me were the sanguinary songs like "There is a fountain filled with blood" and "There is power, power, wonder-working power in the precious blood of the lamb." Miss Jessie Lewis, who played the reed organ, was a teacher in Newton and had to leave town before evening service. I could always hope that I would be invited to play. As a member of the choir I could always sing anyway; but singing was no substitute for both singing and playing. I wanted a thousand tongues and arms and feet to celebrate my great Redeemer's praise! The pastors were young Middle Western Methodists who liked Gospel hymns and who, whether vocally endowed or no, liked to sing. One of them used to bang out upon the very pulpit Bible itself the orgiastic rhythm of "Wonder-Working Power."

By the end of both evening services, I had reached a state of high excitement. Then came the solitary walk back to the farm—somewhat more than a mile along a road from which the street lights soon disappeared, while the houses became infrequent. There were woods on both sides, projecting up from a hollow, in which robbers, murderers, or devils might lurk. I was in terror as I approached the place, and relieved when I had passed it. In passage, I prayed or sang or whistled a hymn, reminding myself of my unseen but ever close Savior who would permit no harm to befall me.

Yet that brief terror was an integral part of the mystical experience ever associated in my mind with the Sunday evening walk—the numinous experience which I craved and cherished. A few nights I had, halfway home, a feeling of levitation—of my feet as not touching the ground, of my body as weightless—a state of transcending the body, which I treasured, feeling it to be some kind of mystical experience—a kind of trance or ecstasy.

I cannot say whether religion or music meant more to me during these solitary and inarticulate years: they were never rivals, never came into opposition. Both were means of self-expression, of asserting my autonomy, identity, what distinguished me as a self from my immediate family, who were neither musical nor more than nominally Christian. They were my ways of participating in the community, serving it in ways I distinctly could. Religion and music also gave me that sense of belonging to worlds which were more than American, of being a member of two international fraternities, about which news were brought me by *Etude,* my musical monthly, by *Zion's Herald,* the excellent Boston Methodist weekly, by the Fundamentalist publications, by the Moody Bible and the David Cook Company of Chicago. Religion was the more ecstatic and metaphysical experience, and the Bible, aided by my New England conscience, was my daily guide. But music, the handmaiden of religion and of culture, was also intense, as well as emotional, and it was an art, and one needed by a Protestant church as well as by the secular village.

My musical history goes back to Waltham. At eight or nine, I had been given piano lessons by an elderly, stout, lame woman. Energetic and motherly, interested in "teaching methods," she was, restrictively, a pedagogue: she did not herself presume to play the piano. This first try at lessons was soon abandoned. I wanted to make music—musical sounds, at least, while my mentor was concerned with the proper position of fingers and wrist, and gave me lessons not on a real piano but on a practice dummy, with keys which produced "ditties of no tone"; she insisted, too, that I practice with a metronome, that my rhythm might attain mechanical exactness. Though I had been started on lessons because my parents had noticed the excitement with which I listened to music, especially the organ in church, and had noticed that I had already begun to play by ear, I discovered that self-expression through music would neither be taught nor permitted by one who taught the New England Conservatory Method.

For several years thereafter, I played the piano by ear, picking out chords I liked, reproducing bits from popular songs and hymns. I forgot how to read music. Then, at Stow, in my early teens, I retaught myself to read the bass clef of hymn tunes. From the hymns, in four-part harmony, I moved to the simpler classics in *Etude* and in the Presser albums of Bach and Handel—and my father's favorite Stephen Foster tunes. But while I taught myself to read music, I still continued to play by ear.

Playing by ear was always severely disapproved of by conscientious New England teachers: no doubt it recalled village fiddlers and other licentious illiterates who grabbed the pleasure of music without shouldering its cross of responsibility. Almost as unsound,

it was taught, was sightreading, a skill impressive to simple auditors, but encouraging pianists to superficiality.

Since the ability to improvise and to read by sight are both
signs of native musical talent (or, at another stage, of musician-
ship) it seems either sad or ludicrous that they should be viewed
with disapproval; but so they were. New Englanders are not, as a
people, lovers, or even likers, of music. Bostonians have made
themselves patrons of music only by being able to see it as "culture" and "discipline."

By my third year in high school, when I could play any "Grade
3" music from the popular musical monthly *Etude*, I had justified
my right to take lessons again, and this time I was fortunate in
my teacher. Miss Grace Sheridan (who came from Hudson to Stow
one day a week, and who was teaching the high school principal,
Mr. Simmons, and a few others), was presumably Irish by origin;
she was, at least, romantic of temperament and sympathetically
though not sentimentally understanding of me. A former student
of piano under John Orth (who had been a student of Liszt's) and
of organ under B. J. Lang, she played both instruments well, with
precision and style, but also with feeling.

Her manner at the piano was visually, as well as acoustically,
striking; for (in a fashion which I soon learned, half-humorously,
to imitate) she swayed back and forth as she played, now bending
forward till her hawk nose had buried itself in the keyboard, now
rearing back her triumphant head—the hands, meanwhile, making
their parallel movements, the dart or swoop, followed by the sudden quick removal of the hand, which reared back on the hinge of
the elbow. Her crossing of left hand over right was also memorable: it was a cherished feature of the style, the high-flying dramatic pianism, in marked contrast to the conservatory low-flying
"touch and technique" with its movement of but wrist and
knuckle.

Her mode of dress was much to my taste: it ran to velvets and
to the grand style, even at her daily work as teacher. When I once
remarked on her costume, she gave me the explanation that she
used up, at teaching, the dresses bought for the concert hall.

Miss Sheridan showed flexibility and good sense in not starting me "all over again from the beginning"—something more conscientious teachers would have done with a self-taught youth—or
even with one who had studied, but with the wrong teacher and
the wrong method. Nor did she, as I had expected, totally deny

me "pieces."I had always a weekly budget of scales and arpeggios, and progressed through several volumes of piano studies (my favorite, those of Moscheles). But I liked this clear, clean drill and specialization provided I wasn't limited to it, and from the start, I wasn't: I was also allowed, as valid assignments, pieces I already owned and had tried to play. In two years, I "read" much. First came Nevin and MacDowell, then Grieg, Chopin (the simpler preludes, nocturnes, mazurkas, waltzes), and Schumann (*Forest Sketches* and other things), often, probably, at my request. Herself, Miss Sheridan excelled at Chopin; but Chopin I could never play with proper digital rapidity; and the feathery ornamentation was as much outside my style as beyond my technique. I was technically able to perform anything which I could musically perceive and feel. Schumann was probably then my favorite composer, at least among the classics.

The piano I played organistically—made it sound as rich, thick, and massive as I could make it. And to aid the acoustic illusion, I made a row of cardboard stops to insert along the keyboard, and (with the aid of a picture in the *Etude* of César Franck at the console of St. Clothilde's in Paris) yanked them out before shifting from soft to loud. My lifelong taste for the organ must have been acquired from the larger, rich, and generally excellent Hock and Hastings instrument in the Waltham Methodist Church. Its appeal for me lay primarily in its being, unlike the piano, an instrument capable of sustained tone; for I liked not only the pipe organ, then found almost entirely in churches, but the humbler and now obsolete instrument made primarily for houses, the reed organ (also known as the parlor organ, the cottage organ, the pump organ, the cabinet organ, and the American organ, the last term used to differentiate it from the analogous British and French keyboard instrument called the harmonium).

I taught myself how to play the pipe organ during my last year in high school. The only local organ, the modest Hock and Hastings of the Unitarian church, lacked a motor; and in order that I might teach myself, Mr. Simmons, the principal of our high school, with touching humility and devotion, crawled through a small door into the organ chamber and pumped it—frequently becoming so absorbed in listening or reverie that he would forget to blow till there came the squeal of the emptying bellows. Before the end of that year, I once had the opportunity to play for Sunday morning service, in the Baptist church at Littleton, an invitation I owed to its regular organist, a woman piano teacher whom I had met at the Christian Endeavor Convention at Stow. My parents were highly skeptical about my attempting this first public performance, but it went off successfully. I was an organist not without honor in Littleton.

3

A College Education: Wesleyan

In the fall of 1916 I entered Wesleyan—*the* Wesleyan University (unlike the very many Wesleyans which bear the prefix of a state—Iowa, Kentucky, or South Dakota). A liberal arts college—in size and social, academic, and football standing comparable to Amherst and Williams—Wesleyan, because of its location in distant Connecticut, was unknown, even by name, to all Massachusettians not professional educators.

The college was chosen for me by my grandmother Dillingham, at the suggestion of her Methodist pastor, a loyal alumnus. Her rationale: my "going away" to college, far enough away so that I could not commute or come home on weekends—the view being that I, particularly, needed to develop the ability to look after myself—to pick up my clothes, to live within my allowance, to learn to get on with other boys. "He who would have friends must show himself friendly," she said.

On college as more than therapeutic—as intellectual, I had no one to counsel me. College education was still, before 1920, the unusual thing among middle-class Yankees. Theirs remained the Yankee feeling of three hundred years before—that gentlemen excepted, college was a professional training for preachers and teachers—those set apart perhaps as much by physical ineptness as by intellectual superiority. Long after my Wesleyan years, I overheard my father telling some callers that it had been necessary to send his son to college because he "couldn't have earned his living by working."

I set out for college without expectations. At least, I could not later remember either wanting or not wanting to go. Some unavowed but strong desire to escape from the constriction of village and family I must have had: yet I lacked any defined hopes of a "better life," or of relief from my aloneness.

The real thing Wesleyan did for me was to give me a friend or two—and many acquaintances, thereby dispelling the chief horror under which I had lived, that of being an anomaly. From Mr. F. J. Simmons, the principal of the high school and the Reverend J. Sidney Moulton, incumbent of the First Parish Church, I should have been able to infer the existence of others like me; but the high school principal and the minister were of removed generations: their kind, I could doubt, might have lapsed.

My new friends were not, by absolute standards, good for me. Neither were they representative of Wesleyan, or by Wesleyan approved. But they gave me the life-giving sense of belonging, and of being able to speak: silent at home, I was astonished to find how much, granted my native tongue, I had to say.

The Wesleyan of my time had little room for "aesthetes" or "intellectuals"—and little tolerance of them.

There was a normative Wesleyan man. His family—still loyally Methodist, though prosperous—lived in New Jersey—at Orange or Upper Montclair. Having come from a prep school, he was already a man of the world, practical in his idealism. His wardrobe included "formals" for the weekend house parties; but his habitual garb, worn to chapel and classes, represented temporary rebellion against that business executive he would presently become. He studied in the new tortoiseshell spectacles. He walked in sneakers, and was shirted in a sweatshirt inked with girls' names and wisecracks: both sneakers and sweatshirt, as soon as bought, must, by ritual law, be dirtied into old clothes. Whatever the weather, he was hatless, but in winter he slopped nonchalantly in unbuckled galoshes, throwing over his sweatshirt a brown leather jacket or— real badge of "conspicuous waste"—a raccoon coat.

Wesleyan was a college of fraternities. Out of the five hundred students, its norm, perhaps fifty were independents, whether by choice or necessity. I came perilously near to being one. A "subfreshman week," held in the spring, gave some fraternities an opportunity to examine, primarily, the youths to enter college in the fall. Through the intermediation of my grandmother's pastor, an alumnus and "brother," I was bidden as subfreshman, and again as entering freshman in the fall, to the scrutinizing hospitality of one very correct fraternity; but, after the rushing season was over, there followed no invitation to join.

The sharp sense of exclusion, and a dim sense of the reasons for it, combined to terrify me. When a humbler fraternity "gave me a bid," I accepted—with relief. With relief, but also with shame that I needed to "belong" and that, needing, I had not made the grade of the status-giving fraternities. The snobbish criteria were as visible to me as I could bear to take in: wealth, family, dress and grooming, ease, assurance. The city-reared had an obvious advantage over the country youths; those with at least a finishing year at prep school over the high school boys.

Within each fraternity, there was a kind of plan of balance. Each delegation (or college class) must muster up a few bookish, scholarly boys, a few star athletes, preferably football players, a few brothers of executive ability (to manage the always precarious finances of the house), a few smooth dancers and mixers—certainly some who were born joiners, and would be active in college organizations like the Y or the glee club. Activities ("extracurricular activities") was the general name for what rated highest. It was the great American game of politics: how to win friends, how to gain, and hold, and augment the power of personality.

I was taken into my fraternity as one whose high grades would pull up its grade average. A secondary claim was my ability to play the piano, for there must be at least one pianist in every delegation to accompany group singing whenever evenings stood in need of being enlivened.

From my fraternity I acquired no feeling of solidarity or community; even though for the last three years I lived at the fraternity house, shared a study with one or two others, and slept in a communal dormitory, where two-decker beds bunked us all.

In these years, sporadic efforts were made to teach me what I certainly needed to be taught—table manners and the rudiments of cleanliness and neatness. I was rebuked for my negligences. In response, I was humiliated and resentful, for I did not know how to do otherwise—had no ability to observe the ways of others and transfer them, with proper adaptations, to myself; and I was supplied no adequate motivation for giving up my anarchy. I was uncouth and proud, not charming or winsome. Yet I would have altered had some brother been able to like me, if not for what I was, then for what I might become.

To the normality around me I made no satisfactory or even consistent adjustment. I oscillated at longer or shorter intervals between wanting to be "regular" and wanting to be "different," conceiving of neither role except superficially. There were days when I could imagine myself "collegiate"; but, alternately, I was the artist—the poet, composer, and concert organist. Subsidiary roles overlapping the artist were those of gentleman and saint—of whom both, as of the artist, the ordinary world was not worthy.

When I felt too persecuted at the House, I could withdraw to one of my cities of refuge—the chapel or the library. The old Gothic library was a sanctuary scarcely invaded except by a few of the professors. The students had their textbooks. The central part—the "nave"—of the library soared unobstructed up to the ceiling; but to its left and right, under the aisles, were rows of galleries (three, above the ground aisle), reached by circular iron stairs. Each of the galleries was divided, by wooden bookstacks at right angles to the gallery rails, into partly enclosed rooms, corners or nooks, often with a table and a chair, sometimes with a green plant. English literature was housed on the ground floor, alphabetically arranged by author; special devotions of mine were the set of Jane Austen and the slim, gray volumes of Emily Dickinson. But my special haunts were higher and more remote: the fine arts section, on the fourth-floor back wall, where there were admirable red-bound German monographs with reproductions of paintings (my favorite, Dürer); then the bays of philosophy and theology on the other side, where, in my sophomore year, I discovered the works of Swedenborg.

In the library I carried on my own private education. But in my first two years, however, I also received instruction from my friend, Benjamin Hezekiah Bissell, who was a junior when I was a freshman. He was a Connecticut Yankee, born in the village of Hebron, soon transplanted, first to Hartford, and then, upon the early death of both parents, to Meriden, where he was brought up by two elderly aunts, one of them bookish, and by his prim mentor, a cultivated Englishman who was organist of Meriden's Episcopal church.

I have no recollection of how we first met. He was not a fraternity man but one of the small group of the not elect who ate at the college refectory, the Common Club. Benny was a real outsider at Wesleyan. He dressed ill, and he was markedly effeminate in his way of walking and his speech; but he read, a rare habit at Wesleyan, where most of the so-called students confined themselves to their assigned textbooks. He had a mind and real courage, determination, and independence. He made no effort to rid himself of his mannerisms or to alter his speech or to adjust his standards and aspirations to those of the "regular Wesleyan men."

My brothers so disapproved of my association with him that I had to meet him clandestinely, a little way off the campus; and even one of my professors, who thought well of me, warned my grandmother that I was keeping unsuitable company. But I disregarded these warnings, knowing that Benny was uniquely, at Wesleyan, the one person from whom I could learn. I was his sole disciple; and he did his best to indoctrinate me with his taste in art and books and his views, Episcopalian, of religion and the Church; and his best was, with me, potent.

Benny's bare, narrow room in the dormitory was, as to its bleakness, rather underlined than relieved by the evidence of aesthetic culture, a series of Perry prints, black and white reproductions of celebrated paintings, attached by clips to a wire suspended the full length of the longest wall. In the second year of our acquaintance, my junior year, he rented a small room in a private house, and there practiced daily on the piano.

His strength, however, lay elsewhere. He was my first real teacher of "philosophy,"of "culture,"a word he had borrowed from Arnold, with whose supercilious mask he identified himself. He read, and gave me to read, the writings of Arnold, Ruskin, and Newman. From these three nineteenth-century masters he had drawn a humanism not wholly unlike what was later to be learned from Irving Babbitt, though distinctly more "idealistic,"that is to say, Romantic.

The dominance among the three was certainly Arnold's; and attributable to Arnold were Benny's chief axioms and even his precise, clipped, mannered way of speaking, so irritating—in part, designedly irritating—to others; his replying to questions with a deliberate "Yes—and no"; his constant inquiry concerning persons and books, whether or not they were "sound." Arnold must also have been his chief model as satirist of the Philistines (i.e., 99 percent of loyal Wesleyan men). But Newman was the model for his prose style, which used to reach me in the form of letters, long essays—epistolary, like St. Paul's, only in their salutation and complimentary close; and it was Newman who developed his talent for persistent, subtle analysis, half philosophical, half psychological.

During the summers, and later, we kept up a copious correspondence. He was my vigilant critic and sometimes my satirist. I used to try to impress him with the booklists I sent him: sometimes as many as twenty books a week I proudly claimed to have read. He disdained the lists, replying, in effect, that if I had really made anything out of what I had read it would show in the quality of my mind and my writing; otherwise it was merely vain statistics.

Benny was, I think, born tired and world-weary. Highly critical and highly civilized, he instinctively took something like Santayana's view of the world as well as Newman's. The "American way of life," with its emphasis on physical vigor and sports, on physical conveniences and comforts, on competition for success, at sports or at grades, on wealth as such and power as such: all struck him as crude, primitive, barbarous. Nor had he any faith in the American, and modern, dogma of progress. He did not believe that bigger was better, or that the practical applications of science had improved the quality of human life.

By comparison with Benny, my professors were scarcely my teachers, though they certainly interested me as persons and types, to be characterized and analyzed.

Wesleyan, then a small college, had a faculty of fifty, most of them full professors who had been appointed at approximately the same time, years ago, and had grown old together. These elder men were more or less withdrawn from the world. Habituated to permanence of tenure, and to teaching chiefly so-called students, youths who had come to college to acquire social smoothness and prestige and to make connections which would help into, and up in, business, most of these professors went through their stated duties rather perfunctorily; lectured from yellow notes. And, though, by pedagogic standards better teachers, the younger professors were too commonplace as persons and minds, too patently "talking down," to command respect.

The most learned of my professors, the incumbent of the chair of Greek, was the least effectual as an instructor. At home—what with his slow, cautious utterance, and the softness of his voice— Professor Heidel had given up competing with his nimble-witted, articulate wife and his hearty, shrewish mother-in-law. But in the classroom, almost equally, he lacked the sense of having anything to say which anyone wanted to hear or felt the need to know. So he mumbled softly, to himself.

Morally impressive, certainly, was his not minding, or not suffering more, from being so ineffectual; he conveyed the sense of loyalty to some unnamed cause; he never seemed crude or cheap. But, as certainly, he was unsuited to teaching—at least, to teaching undergraduates; and I was glad to learn, some years thereafter that he had been put, by Carnegie money, on a research professorship.

Some of the older professors were eccentrics, each in his own mode.

Professor Mead headed the Department of English Language and Composition, a department divided from that of literature by virtue of his incompatibility with the more popular and admired Winchester, the critic and essayist. An odd collection of courses was Mead's: sophomore composition, Old English, which I studied with him. Sometimes he taught Chaucer. Perhaps also there was, in the college catalog, a titular offering of Celtic, at which Mr. Mead was adept. All the professors who were "scholars," but especially Mr. Mead, liked to keep, in the catalog a long repertory of specialized courses, under which, annually, the legend would read, "Not offered this year."

Mead was perhaps the most whimsical and stylized of the faculty eccentrics: his habits seemed partly self-parody; partly expressive of the contempt he felt toward the world generally and especially "Wesleyan men"; partly pranks by which to amuse himself. He saw himself, undoubtedly, as an ironist, a scholar and gentleman living among barbarians, and I did not begrudge his partially illusory comfort.

As if to compensate for the smallness of his classes, he had an uncommonly large office. His compulsory course, Sophomore Composition, required the writing of three essays a semester—each to be slipped under Mr. Mead's door at a precise day and hour and later to be made the subject of a conference. When, keeping my appointment, I knocked on the door, I would hear, as from far within a high small voice uttering what I later learned to interpret as "Come," though what the voice really said was "Coom." I entered, but seeing no one, would look around, bewildered and embarrassed. Gradually, as I became accustomed to the dimness and the clutter, I would grow aware of sharp eyes peering at me, amused at my confusion; and then I would see the neat little figure of Dr. Mead, sitting quietly on the floor behind a great dictionary or half hidden behind a green baize screen—pink, but puckered of face, a monkey mask—skeptical and quizzical.

The professor of Romance languages, Oscar Kuhns, was a strange and touching figure. A childlike innocent, he seemed an inevitable bachelor; but, like all the other scholarly professors, he was actually married—even somehow had begotten a son. His wife, a sensible, practical woman, taller and larger framed than her husband, treated him as a child, without contempt. The pair were frequently to be seen on the streets of Middletown as Mrs. Kuhns, capacious bag in vigorous hand, set out to do her household shopping. Keeping firm hold of the professor with her second hand, she steered him along, while he, like an inquisitive little boy, now gaped at something across the street, now peered behind him, or "thought beautiful thoughts."

According to college rumor, Kuhns had once been a remarkable scholar, but had overstudied, and had a breakdown from which he had never wholly recovered. At the time I knew him, he had abandoned scholarly publication and was happily busy writing "helpful" little books, such as *The Peaceful Life* and *A One-Sided Autobiography* (the story of his life among books). His colleagues were satirical of the rapidity with which he composed these books and of their sentimentality, but gently satirical—and he was unaware of their judgment.

When he countered me in the corridor of Fisk Hall—in those noisy, crowded intervals between classes when just to make one's way was difficult—he would smile radiantly and quote a fine verse in Latin or Italian: perhaps "In la sua voluntade e nostra pace."

The most solid and the least eccentric of my teachers was Caleb T. Winchester. He had been much admired by older Wesleyan men; and he was, or had been, widely known outside Wesleyan also. Not a Ph.D., he had, like Kittredge and Babbitt of Harvard, done more writing and publishing than his colleagues equipped with German doctorates. With Kittredge, he had been coeditor of Ginn's excellent Athenaeum series of annotated literary texts. He had written a *Principles of Literary Criticism* (halfway between the old and the New), which, as some of us students were aware, had been translated into Japanese; and he published a book on the English essayists, and a biographical and critical *Wordsworth*.

Winchester was a man of admirable dignity and presence. The general image was that of Matthew Arnold: iron-gray hair, still rather copious; side-whiskers without beard; steel-rimmed pince-nez suspended from a black cord, to be set upon his Roman nose when he read. His habitual garb was the black frock coat, with waistcoat and striped gray trousers. About this garb there was something ritual and stylized: already slightly archaic, it had been conspicuously adopted, or continued, by C. T. W. as befitting his conception of the professor and as suitable and becoming to him, a sixty-five-year-old New England gentleman. It was a more specific distinction of Winchester's appearance that his clothes were tailored, of excellent material; that he was groomed and immaculate; that his cuffs, emerging slightly from his sleeves as he sat at the seminar table, were gold studded; that his handkerchiefs were crisp linen.

I was too young and crude then to do justice to Winchester's qualities of mind, character, and taste; something brilliant even if hysterical would have better served my desires. In characterizing Winchester, one must use the balanced style of Dr. Johnson: he was serious without being pompous; earnest without being priggish; careful of facts and distinctions without being pedantic. If he had a central passion, it was a passionate desire for balance, equilibrium, rounded development, the Hellenic ideal (to which, with Arnold, he thought inadequate justice done by Yankee Hebraism).

It was Winchester's real distinction that his mind was closely integrated with his character. From one so solid and massive, dogmatic convictions and pronouncements might be expected. But they were infrequent. Rather he could be, and often was, tentative, speculative, inquiring.

Teaching Emerson and Lowell, he would contrast his own earlier interpretations and estimates of the poems with his present judgment, though implying, in the process, his doubt about that judgment too. Large, sweeping generalizations he felt to be as emotionally crude as untrue: he wished to define, qualify, restrict, reserve. For example: such a poet was, perhaps, the best English songwriter in quatrains between 1660 and 1675. Yet Winchester's was a precision not of historical scholarship as such (the domain of his squirrel-like rival, Mr. Mead) but of literary judgment. With rarely combined delicacy and vigor, he represented the critical study of literature in a day, and at a place, where science and historical method seemed the only two really modern academic competences.

I minored in English; I majored in Latin. My chief professor in that major was Karl Pomeroy Harrington, and it was he, among my teachers, whom I knew best and least, for though we got on well enough superficially, at any depth we distrusted each other— or at least felt an imperfect sympathy.

Unlike Winchester, he had studied at a German university; but, unlike Mead and others of his generation, he had returned to his native land without a doctorate. This means, I take it, that he was half a scholar, after the technical style of the Germans, and half some kind of humanist and artist. He was a fellow organist. During his years at the University of Berlin, he played for the American Church; and all through his Wesleyan career he was the organist of Middletown's First Methodist Church. He was also an active and proud member of the Appalachian Club, composed of mountain climbers and trail makers. Probably he saw himself as a Renaissance man, the universal man, scholar and artist, the grandiose role to which I too aspired; but, if so, he suffered from having, so far as I could discern, no hierarchy within his spectrum of values and activities.

In the past, he had done some good scholarly work, notably, as editor of the Roman Elegiac Poets; but research did not appear really to engage him. When I called upon him at the spacious but dusty and fusty office, he seemed always glad to be interrupted in whatever unnamed book-work he was engaged at. Sometimes we talked about the cause of the classics, already a cause on the defensive. I was president of the Classical Club; and I had worked up the standard arguments for keeping Latin in the curriculum, the chief of which was that one could not write English well or read Milton intelligently without a sense of Latin syntax and the Latin background of English words. But mainly we just chatted. I needed an intellectual father; but Harrington was not concerned to accept the office; nor did he provide me with a model of the classicist as a mature man whose intellectual and spiritual life had been enriched and fortified by the years he had given to the classics.

During the Wesleyan period my sense for language was dominant. In my first three years, I continued the Latin I had begun in Waltham and Stow, and began French (of which I had but a year) and Greek. I could write and speak, elementarily, German—chiefly in consequence of the conversation I often had with "Frau," the German cook at our fraternity—and won the prize in German. My Latin included, I remember with pleasure, a semester of writing Latin prose, well taught by a Canadian, Frank Nicholson, the dean of the college; such a course must have been a late survival. To learn to write Latin verse or to speak Latin I lacked the opportunity, and I regret these absences. I loved the sound of Latin.

I link together my two early developments: language (especially poetry) and music. It was primarily the sound of language I loved. Conceptual, semantic, philosophical interests all developed later; and, when they did, my love for language declined: I had no wish to speak facilely even though incorrectly on trivial matters in several languages; and to speak and write my own with precision and distinction seemed difficult enough. I did not care to know how to say, "Pass me the butter" in four or five languages, I used to think to myself and sometimes say to others.

With Professor Harrington I read the Roman philosophers, Lucretius, Cicero (*De officiis*), and Seneca, and the Latin poets, especially Horace and Catullus. (I much preferred Catullus: he and
Lucretius and Virgil were the Romans who seemed to me real
poets.) I was also assigned Tyrrell's *Anthology of Latin Poetry*,
including excerpts from early poets like Ennius to silver Latin poets like Statius and late Latin poets—Ausonius, Claudian, Pruden-
tius—the first Christian poet—and Boethius.

Something surely was to be learned—surely must have been
learned—from such professors of the humanities as I have characterized. Yet, on the whole, I was unaffected, except negatively, by
these my official teachers. It was a benefit, I then thought, that
they left me to my own self-educative devices and didn't pry or
meddle. At a later time, I felt resentment that Wesleyan had so
little bothered to educate me, that no one of my teachers had
really sought to win my friendship and allegiance, but then, without knowledge of any superior education to be had, I took this gap
between the world of professors and the world of students as natural law. And, since they weren't interested in teaching what I
wanted to learn, I attended their lectures with ritual docility and
then—on my own—tried to learn what I wanted.

No serious effort was ever made to teach me to think. Professor Armstrong's semester course in formal logic (with Jevons as
text) brought me an A, but I may well have memorized the syllo-
gisms; and, furthermore, Armstrong's grades, by student rumor,
were reported to be even less predictable than those of other teachers. His habit, the rumor reported, was to throw a batch of examinations down the hall stairs, grading them by the step on which
they landed. In his History of Philosophy, Armstrong read lectures
from yellowed notes, but assigned no readings in the great philosophers whom he summarized and evaluated. I left Wesleyan unread
in any philosopher.

Other potent lacks in my education were mathematics, applied science, philosophy, history. From Professor Dutcher's famous and compulsory course in English history, taken in my freshman year, I learned nothing which I either could, or cared to,
retain. The professor compensated for his prissiness of manner and
diction by his sadistic habits of ridiculing students and of giving
unannounced written tests aimed wholly at "catching"the student,
and, therefore, not at the essentials, but at unrelated detail. In his
violently precise way, Mr. Dutcher was, doubtless, a brilliant as
well as learned and efficiently purposed lecturer; but he gave me

absolutely no conception of history, or of England, or of why one should study either: he not only lacked but felt superior to any philosophy of history.

Three full year courses in physical science were required of all Wesleyan men. I at once met and evaded the requirement by electing two years of geology and one of Evolution and Genetics. These courses were chosen, negatively, because they involved no laboratory work, no revolting dissection of frogs, no chemical stinks: positively, because dealing with grandiose perspectives—they seemed, so far as sciences were capable of being—both poetic and philosophic.

The first geology course, with the tiny, aged, and fragile William North Rice, celebrated, at least by Wesleyan, for having reconciled science and religion, tolerably gratified my expectations. Rice was a man of general culture and intelligence, like Winchester, and of expository skill, like T. H. Huxley; and in his lectures, fact, idea, form, and style coexisted in some niceness of balance.

But the younger scientists were, personally and professionally, of a different cast—specialists, without Rice's perspective or his expository art. The coadjutor in geology was an earnest, socially awkward little man, a Baptist and probably a native of Iowa, Kansas, or Nebraska. Both he and the young biologist who taught Evolution doubtless felt superior to W. N. Rice as to some archaic precursor of the scientist, and took their very inability to arrange, present, and interpret as marks of their dedication to scientific scholarship, to pure science; but a youthful humanist could scarcely be expected to share their high self-esteem.

I took pleasure in the lantern slides which illustrated the lectures, showing, sometimes in color, the prehistoric world of dinosaurs and brontosaurs, slides based upon "the careful reconstruction of scientists," and by the contrast between these picturesque, fanciful worlds, these fairy-tale nightmares, and the angular bodies and minds of the matter-of-fact scientific lecturers, I was amused. Having escaped from the Fundamentalism of Stow I felt no disturbance at the collision between Genesis and Evolution. But, especially in my last years at Wesleyan, I was hostile to the liberal Protestant reduction of religion, to its general translation of myth and mysticism into reason, common sense, and cheerful kindness. I felt it absurd that these men, unable to believe the Bible, should then devise their own extravagant myth of how the world began. The sundry theories of evolution interested me, as any theories did; but I took them to be modern speculation rather than history or science.

The First World War mildly and briefly interrupted my college schedule. In my second year, required military training was introduced; and in my junior year—from September to December 1918—I was a duly sworn-in member of the U.S. Army, a private in the SATC. This was a pathetic and comic episode. I had no one to help me think honestly what stand to take. My grandmother Dillingham was patriotic in a conventional way, admired "real men," liked uniforms and the idea of drill as discipline; was proud, as was my father, of my being "in the service"; proud when I came home at Christmas time in ill-fitting khaki; proud, later, of my "discharge papers," which were kept in the safe deposit box, to be shown proudly to my future children.

But nothing in me responded to this set of notions. So far as I could see, the "war effort" of my elders, at home or at college, amounted to a pious humbuggery. The older professors were set to teaching, quite academically, sections of a course in War Aims. Wesleyan's president, Dr. William Arnold Shanklin, a clerical sentimentalist and rhetorician, used to inveigh in chapel, perhaps even in his pulpit prayers, against "William the Damned" (i.e., the kaiser). I must have had inclinations toward religious pacifism, but I finally set them down as personal, as simply expressive of my own temperamental incapacity for physical combat.

Certainly I no more credited the "wickedness"of the Germans than I believed in the fairy tales of science. For one thing, my German-educated professors were obviously unable to believe that the kind, culture-loving dreamers they had known could have turned into goose-stepping Prussians. For another, I didn't trust the American patriots, who seemed to me just my old acquaintances, the unimaginative, sadistic Philistines, playing some kind of game of kick football, which though they took it earnestly, could scarcely matter to artists and philosophers. The war propaganda seemed part of the general American setup, the setup so faithfully, so nauseatingly mirrored at Wesleyan, by "Wesleyan men": a system in which religion, philosophy, the arts, and friendship were chiefly left to women, but which, patronizingly, pretended to sympathize with these "higher values"—played upon their credit, and parroted their phrases.

So hopelessly outnumbered and outshouted by my relatives and my brothers and other "Wesleyan men," I never considered speech in protest; but at least I felt no need to be overtly or verbally patriotic when, to my perception, patriotism was the then current name for almost all which was wrong with America.

Strangely, I did well in the courses set me during my brief period in uniform: won an A both in the Principles of Economics and in a specialized course in Railroad Transportation. But it was a delight to me to decline my instructor's invitation to enroll in a second semester devoted to another mode of transportation, perhaps marine, and to return to my characteristic pursuits. During the second semester of my junior year, I elected none but courses in Greek, Latin, German, and English.

In my time, Wesleyan had no departments of music and the fine arts. To represent these interests, a younger fraternity brother of mine, Paul Vaka (my disciple as I had been Bissell's), and I founded a Fine Arts Club, so-called, though Vaka and I, both musicians, knew little of painting and architecture; in this club, which assembled a few other young men of mildly aesthetic concern, we had the collaboration of Middletown's cultivated ladies—the wife of the dean of Berkeley Divinity School and the two or three faculty wives who sang lieder

All through my Wesleyan days, I dabbled at writing. As a sophomore, I published a few poems in the Wesleyan *Literary Monthly*, discontinued with the advent of the war. In my senior year, with the mild encouragement of Professor Harrington, and my friend Bissell, now a graduate student at Yale, I submitted a collection of poems for publication in the Yale Younger Poets, a series just inaugurated. The poems were jumbled echoes from the Romantic poets—from Poe, Emerson, Shelley, and Keats: crude performances. In these last years at Wesleyan, the imagist movement was in progress; and Professor Winchester bought for his bookshelves the thin jade-green volumes of Amy Lowell's poems and her critical book, *Tendencies in Contemporary Poetry*. And I, who read uncritically both the new and the old, imitated free verse, but not more intelligently than I had Keats.

With a little more success, I attempted criticism. During my senior year, I wrote a series of thirty essays on American literature, including the "new poets," Frost, Robinson, Amy Lowell, as well as Emily Dickinson and William Vaughn Moody—my medium of publication the *Waltham Free-Press-Tribune*, the daily newspaper owned and edited by my distant relative, Alexander Starbuck.

Though at Wesleyan, I thought of myself, grandiosely, as theologian and musician, and a man of letters, by my contemporaries

I was certainly, and properly, reduced to the specialty of musician; and my daily service as the chapel organist of Wesleyan was my chief means of enjoying and serving the college community.

Already, in the middle of my freshman year, I possessed self-confidence enough to have applied for a vacant post as organist and choirmaster, at the Congregational Church of East Hampton, ten miles from Middletown—a post regularly occupied by a Wesleyan undergraduate of musical talent. I won the post; and, through my junior year, I regularly left Middletown by train for East Hampton each Saturday afternoon, conducted choir rehearsal Saturday evening, played for morning and evening services on Sunday, and returned to Middletown early Monday morning. These weekends did much to make my early college years livable, for they gave me the feeling that I was of consequence, not a mere college student.

The East Hampton organ, located in the traditional loft at the opposite end from the pulpit, was a simple, limited, two-manual instrument, with a pedal board of less than two octaves, inadequate for the performance of Bach or any of the standard organ repertory. But I was accustomed to playing a reed organ, to adapting simple keyboard music like Handel's "Largo" or "Sarabande," to using transcriptions, to extemporizing a pedal part out of the bass of the keyboard score, to all kinds of extemporizing, including interludes. Hence, I found no difficulty and considerable interest in my work at the organ, including the accompaniment of the choir and of the hymns, the music of which I took seriously, which I aimed to have a share in choosing.

The direction of a choir was an experience requiring pedagogic skill and especially tact, for my singers were all untrained and unpaid, and all, or almost all, were middle-aged and the voices were neither strong nor good. The special problem in any similar American choir was to find a tenor or tenors: the genuine article simply does not occur among Yankees; and the choirmaster has to make do with baritones who force their voices upward.

The choir sang an anthem on Sunday morning, simple things without solo parts of any length. On special occasions, I could summon the help of one trained singer in East Hampton—a middle-aged contralto who would sing "O Rest in the Lord" from *Elijah* or "He Was Despised" from the *Messiah*.

When I gave, as I occasionally did, an afternoon organ recital, I could call upon two trained sopranos from Middletown, wives of my professors. And I was assisted by one or more of these ladies when I presented, with my choir, a cantata I myself, self-trained in harmony, had composed. It was called *The Holy City*, and based entirely on verses from the book of Revelation, in which, from boyhood, I had taken pleasure for its sonority and its mystery.

In the middle of my sophomore year, in 1917, I became, with the departure for the war of the then organist, the college organist of Wesleyan—the student who played for the compulsory daily morning chapel service, fifteen minutes in length, which was conducted more or less in turn by the older and more pious professors. I had a prelude and postlude to play, and two hymns, those selected by the officiating professor. These hymns were generally not to my taste: were too sentimental, both in words and music.

The second semester of my sophomore year I had weekly organ lessons from a master I much respected, Joseph Clair Beebe of New Britain. With him I studied Bach seriously, starting with the trio sonatas (which then seemed to me like exercises) and ascending to the Toccata and Fugue in D minor, which I played with tolerable precision and dexterity but which chiefly delighted me because I could end with what was to me a supreme delight, the "full organ"—in this case, the full organ of a three-manual organ, made by the Austin Company in Hartford.

I was paid something for my services as college organist, which continued till my graduation, in 1920. I was paid also for my work at East Hampton. But I was proud when, at the end of my junior year, I was invited to become, in the autumn, organist of the large and fashionable, or at least correct, Middletown church, the South Congregational. My weekly wage was raised from five to eight dollars; I had but one service to play (there was, in this city church, only a morning service); and, instead of a volunteer choir, I had a paid quartet to direct, the contralto of which, Miss Katherine Bacon, of a well-to-do local family, was both a lady and a New York trained singer.

South Church was the height of my musical career. I got on well with the minister and with the music committee, headed by a local banker, quite the gentleman. Indeed, with all ministers I got on well, partly, perhaps because, unlike most organists, I listened critically but appreciatively to their sermons. Then, at South Church, I had at my disposal an organ far more to my taste than the newer one in the Wesleyan chapel; for this one was built in the nineteenth century, by Steere and Roosevelt, to be a real organ, not an imitation of an orchestra: it was solid in its tonal architecture—diapason, reeds, mixtures—and rich in tone.

My main achievement at South Church was to set up a series of musical vespers which I proposed and arranged for the spring of 1920, my last year at Wesleyan. They were held each Sunday afternoon in Lent, ending with Palm Sunday. The program was a concert: an organ recital, interspersed with solos—Miss Bacon singing Gounod's "O Divine Redeemer" or Franck's "Panis Angelicus," or a violin solo, or a piano solo: at one of these vespers, Annette Dacier, my French-Canadian girlfriend, played Bach's Chromatic Fantasy and Fugue.

For my own contribution: it was the accepted ceremonial of organists at this period to open their recitals with something by Bach, the only organ composer before the nineteenth century that was played. Like most of my elders, I did not, at that time, find Bach's music (generally thought of as limited to fugues) to be really musical: his work seemed archaic, dry, and exercise-like. But I dutifully began each organ program with a prelude and fugue.

The organ and church music, though partly delightful to me because they served the cause of religion, were yet delightful also for their art and for enabling me to serve the college and the church communities in which I felt otherwise so much an outsider. But religion, my form of metaphysics, was even a deeper concern, binding me in my aloneness to Ultimate Reality, to God.

I was on my way to Christian Platonism and to the Episcopal Church, into which I was confirmed, at Princeton, in 1926. But there were obstacles to the sudden shift from the Fundamentalism and pietism of my Stow religion, so strongly Protestant, to a church I viewed (partly under Benny's influence) as Catholic; and my Methodistically religious and favorite grandmother opposed this conversion. So I was intermediately, by way of transition, a Swedenborgian.

The specific versions of Protestantism offered by my college— "Wesleyan religion"—a Protestantism urban and liberal, repelled me as makeshift and not really religious: whether that of our venerable professor of geology, William North Rice, who had reconciled religion and evolution, or down to Professor Hewitt, an earnest humanitarian as well as pedagogically adept teacher of Greek and Latin. I felt consistently hostile to, even contemptuous of, the inch-by-inch surrender of religion to science and the higher criticism. The muscular young Christians, the YMCA men, I found even more offensive. In my freshman year, I attended a Y meeting or two, only to be disgusted by the combination of sentimentalism

and humanitarianism, of anti-intellectualism and antiecclesiasti-
cism. The Y seemed to be a rival to "the churches," and, by its
absence of dogma and worship and its segregation of college young
men from the rest of the community, at once crude and snobbish.

Soon I came to feel the limitations of Methodism and of Protestantism generally. *Protestant* became—and long remained for
me—a pejorative term. My glimpses of New England and mid-
Western Unitarianism had made me aware of the negative, the
parasitic, character of liberal religion, of religion which preached
its noncredo against orthodoxy and scorned pious practices lest
they include some element of superstition. For my part I desired
to say, "I believe."

In my sophomore year, quite on my own, I came upon
Swedenborg, whose massive *Works* occupied a shelf in the college
library's wrought-iron balcony devoted to metaphysics. During his
life, the Baron Swedenborg, whose dates are 1688 to 1772, published his *Opera* in Latin at his own expense and sent free copies
to the English bishops and to the universities, including Harvard
College. After the Revelator's death, his followers—commonly
well-to-do but, whether so or not, missionaries of the printed word,
"people of the book"—sent free sets of the writings to all universities and colleges. And so Wesleyan possessed a set.

I desired to retain my faith in the Bible as the word of God
without having to defend the Bible in toto, or as science and history. This Swedenborg enabled me to do; for he taught that the
literal history in the Bible began only with the life of Abraham,
and he rejected the full inspiration of the New Testament
Epistles—not merely that of St. James, which Luther disposed of
as "an Epistle of straw," but the letters of St. Paul as well. Like the
Christian Platonists of Alexandria, Swedenborg believed that the
word of God, contained in the Bible, possessed—over and above its
literal sense—a "spiritual sense" and a "celestial sense." His basic
works were exegeses of these higher senses—notably the *Arcana
Coelestia* (expounding Genesis and Exodus) and two works on the
Apocalypse—which, with the four Gospels, constituted for
Swedenborg the plenary word of God in the New Testament.

It was Swedenborg who made it possible for me to pass from
a Fundamentalist view of the Bible to a higher critical view without strain or tension—for me to take the early parts of Genesis as
myth without feeling that I had rejected the word of God. And he
introduced me to the whole study of spiritual symbolism—for
which he had his own fixed system, his "Science of Correspon-

dences." But his more learned followers saw the connection of his system with other symbolic systems.

Swedenborg was salutary fare for a dreamy youth. Though himself a mystic, he was a mystic who, till his fifties, had been a scientist, and the character of his writing, his style, is dry and gritty, not "poetical." He writes as a scientist intent on closely observing and accurately reporting facts, things "seen and heard in the spiritual world," and he reasons, dryly, on the basis of those facts. He was the first philosopher, or philosophical theologian, whom I had ever read. And it was he chiefly who turned me from being a pietist into an amateur theologian and student of mysticism, hermeneutics, and comparative religion.

I was not merely a reader of Swedenborg, however, but, ecclesiastically minded as I was, I "joined" the Church of the New Jerusalem, founded not by the seer but by English adherents to his system; I was confirmed into its membership in my senior year at Wesleyan.

This senior year had its modest secular triumphs. I was early elected to Phi Beta Kappa. I was president of the Classical Club and the Fine Arts Club. I was organist of Middletown's South Church as well as chapel organist of Wesleyan. And, at commencement, I was class poet.

Now came suddenly the stringent need to settle on a profession. To the ministry I had not been encouraged by my pastors and other ecclesiastical seniors—doubtless because I was judged too religious, too impractical, insufficiently social. Of music I had of course thought; but for a man, music as a profession still seemed improper. Well, why not, then, teach the classics, in which I had majored? No. I found that I wanted to reach and influence more than the few specialists who would major in Greek and Latin. Thus, by the process of negation, I settled for teaching English, i.e., culture in general.

But did I know how to teach? I went to the Wesleyan library for three or four standard texts on the principles and problems of education, only to have my anxiety augmented. I read of the taxing situations to arise in the classroom and how one should handle them. Not dissenting from the solutions, I wondered how I could possibly remember, in the excitement of a classroom crisis, those wise prescriptions handed out by the teachers of teachers.

4

Graduate Studies: Harvard and Princeton

In the fall of 1921 I entered the Graduate School of Harvard: but this chapter properly begins when Benny Bissell, recently discharged from service in the First World War, began work for a doctorate in English at Yale; for it was he, my first and only Wesleyan mentor, who made it a matter not of routine, but of indispensable "soundness,"that I should take a doctorate.

Several times I journeyed from Middletown to New Haven to visit my friend and be impressed by what he used to call "pure research." I attended at least one lecture by Dean Wilbur Gross, later governor of Connecticut; and I was taken to view the seminar room in which the great Albert Stanborough Cook, Professor of Old English (but also teacher of Dante, Ruskin, the theory of poetry, and the "first principles" of both scholarship and morality) held his famous classes. I was properly impressed, even by the vacant and silent room dedicated to the Higher Study of literature.

Bissell's favorite pose, during these visits from his junior, was that of one initiating a novice into solemn rites and mysteries. He was careful always to give me the sense that more was withheld than revealed and to impart a doubt whether my intellectual capacities were equal to the severe exactions made upon graduate students, especially as they engaged in their pure research.

In his own instance, when the time arrived, he accepted a dissertation topic obviously handed out to him by the eighteenth-century scholar, Chauncey Brewster Tinker, whom he greatly admired as Professor Cook's successor: less ponderous, more an urbane man of the world—and a High Churchman as well. Bissell had fun in talking impressively about his topic, referring to it as

"A Study in American Exoticism"; but the fun was thin compensation for the labor so irrelevant to my friend's real talents as his dissertation turned out to be—the collection of references to the American Indian in eighteenth-century English literature.

When my turn came, I went to Harvard for a year, and for two years more to Princeton, passing up Yale. I must have been partly motivated by recalcitrance against Bissell's pontificality but also by my need to make up for not having gone to Harvard College as an undergraduate.

This move to Cambridge was certainly not urged by my knowing the names and reputations of the illustrious professors with whom, that very rich year, I studied—F. N. Robinson, Kittredge, John Livingstone Lowes, Bliss Perry, and Irving Babbitt—for I was ignorant of them all. This good fortune must have originated from the more or less fixed requirements for the master's degree. My courses were four: Chaucer, Shakespeare, and the Romantic movement—all of which ran through the year. The fourth was compounded of a semester with Perry on Carlyle and a comparative literature course on the Renaissance taught—chiefly as a seminar—by Lowes. Though I did creditably in all my courses, I was positively engaged only by Babbitt's.

George Lyman Kittredge's English 2, a celebrated Shakespeare course primarily for undergraduates, I found the least profitable, and Kittredge himself I found a combination of pedant, tyrant, and exhibitionist, whose tricks and pranks and sadisms were not amusing. He had no method of teaching and no theory of literature, indeed avoided both the consecutive and the rounded. Four plays were taught each semester—*Hamlet* and *Lear* among them—but the plays were never dealt with as wholes. Handsome Kittredge strode handsomely into the room; asked, "Well, gentlemen, what questions?" By questions he meant minute inquiries about the meaning of a line or a word. Most of us were too intimidated to speak up, and on a few occasions no one did, whereupon our teacher said, "Well, gentlemen, if there are no questions, the class is dismissed." At best, the class hours consisted of a series of glosses on Rolfe's expurgated text: a series of notes on words or allusions; their choice, a matter of chance and caprice. The old professor was not, like some Shakespeareans, either fantastic or obsessed; he was obviously sensible and Yankee. But I found neither in his lectures nor in his books any real sensibility, originality, or wisdom.

Although antipodal to Kittredge, Bliss Perry was scarcely more profitable. His history, then unfamiliar to me, had included a period as editor of the *Atlantic Monthly*, once a literary and serious magazine: for the second half of the nineteenth century doubtless American culture at its best. But the Perry whom I knew seemed without tone or distinction or acuteness—all blandness, blur, and amiability. He was a "familiar essayist," while I was in search of a critic or a philosopher. Nor did I think better of him when the denunciations of Carlyle I offered in my class essays were not argued back but instead highly praised.

Diminutive Lowes, birdlike of movement, was doubtless keen, as he was certainly learned; but he was an impressionist, and his *Road to Xanadu* I found lacking in theory, and I judged its style "literary" in the worst sense—a mosaic of such familiar quotations as the "sea-change" from *The Tempest*. Yet, in his own fashion, Lowes cared for literature—not otiose praise to bestow upon a professor of English. He took interest even in the poetry of the twentieth century, and wrote a book inspired by the vers libre of Amy Lowell.

Babbitt's course on the Romantic movement I elected on the amusing misapprehension that the Romanticists, whose poetry I knew in part, were spirits like myself—"idealists," and that the course would be a defense of their position against Philistinism— to use the term I had acquired from Benny, who had acquired it from Matthew Arnold, who had acquired it from Heine. When I found Babbitt attacking Romanticism and using "Romanticist" as a term of opprobrium, I was more confused than offended.

In any conventional sense, Babbitt was not a good teacher; he was something better or worse; better, of course. For the first two months I felt myself being whirled about, unable to get my bearings, baffled by Babbitt's whole intellectual position as well as his classroom method, which was to plunge *in medias res* and to end whenever the bell rang.

Irving Babbitt in his classroom was an experience not before encountered nor ever to be forgotten. Before me sat an alert, powerfully built figure with massive head, carved in shrewd lines, and with piercing eyes that contradicted his gray hair and stoop of shoulders. About him there was nothing genteel or—as I had learned the outward and visible signs—gentlemanly. A green bag, stuffed and bulging, accompanied his precipitate entrance; its contents, in the shape of books and disorderly papers, were hastily unloaded upon the desk, and the discourse began. The lecture followed no outline. There were no clerical or professional firstlies and thirdlies, indeed no discernible sequence; instead there was a torrential flow of enunciations, theses, antitheses, and epigrams. Frequently the discourse would find momentary interruption while the sage announced, "I choose an illustration at random." The example culled from, Boileau or Mencken, or jaggedly cut from a newspaper or a current magazine, perhaps *Photoplay*, proved so apposite as to startle us listeners with uncoached amusement, and in our laughter Babbitt frankly and heartily joined.

According to the Harvard catalog, Babbitt was allocated to the Department of French; and his examples came frequently from the literature in which he was presumably a specialist. But the citations were translated, as though the matter in point lay in message, not in style; and the quotations—innumerable in the course of an hour—came indifferently from other literatures: from English and American, from German or Italian, from Latin and Greek—now and then from Chinese or Pali or Sanskrit. Nor were his citations restricted to belles lettres. The philosophers and the theologians appeared familiarly at the beck of his easy wand, as did the historians and the scientists.

Unprecedented and puzzling was the familiarity with which Babbitt invoked these great names. They were treated without the ceremony which I had supposed the due of authors in print—and in handsome and shelf-filling sets, men who had written "works" and appeared in histories. In this classroom they all met with the same vigorous scrutiny one might administer to contemporary authors. Our teacher treated the illustrious dead to no uncritical deference. He commended, he censured, he mixed praise and blame; but—and this was the surprising effect of his irreverence—he brought the dead to life.

Drama invaded the classroom; we who listened saw visions; these books, these sets, these works all harbored blood. These volumes fought one another. There was a battle of the books going on now; not merely in Swift's time, but always. Old errors slumbered for a time but periodically awoke: the heresy of yesterday became the novelty, the new thought of today. Similarly the orthodox sages and saints of former times encompassed us and our contemporaries, encompassed us about as so many witnesses and guardians. Athanasius—or Irving Babbitt—was not really, whatever the appearance—a solitary champion *contra mundum*. Each stood alone in his moment, perhaps; but against the aberrations of the moment we were to oppose the great tradition of which these isolated figures were local representatives.

I could gather that Babbitt, as, leoninely restless, he crouched at his desk—ready, it seemed, to spring—was addressing his blows, thrusts, thumps at some unseen assailant, some enemy who was menacing the walls of the state, nay—more ominous—threatening the disruption of civilization. That Babbitt was a great idealist, a champion of morality and culture I could not doubt; and as one who had waged valiant battle, as an undergraduate, in defense of our classical heritage, I was assured by his attitude toward the ancients. But never before had I encountered "classic"and "Romantic" as antinomies; and to hear the latter denounced as false prophesy was a long-standing pain.

Nor did the "transvaluation of values" stop here: at the Babbittian assault, many terms and many causes gave up the ghost. Once so proud of my effervescent "enthusiasm,"I grew so ashamed of thing and name that to this day I cannot write the word without enclosing it in prophylactic quotes. Humanitarianism, and aestheticism—they were other demons to which I, unwitting, had tendered the hospitality due angelic visitants.

Though I could not tell the day and the hour, I, like many others in that classroom, experienced conversion. Obediently—indeed with a zealot's ardor—I burned what once I had adored. Not content with immolating Shelley and Poe, Wordsworth and Emerson, I turned my fierce scrutiny upon the composers. I closed my albums of MacDowell and Grieg, of Chopin and Schumann and Schubert. From being the hero, Wagner became the villain of music.

To Babbitt and his "philosophy,"as one came to discern it, one must have possessed the lethargy of a graduate student to remain indifferent. His challenge divided the class into the receivers and the deniers; and upon the former group his influence was hypnotic.

Babbitt indoctrinated the faithful, of that there can be no doubt. To advocates of the university as an intellectual cafeteria, this admission would be sufficiently damnatory of the teacher; and it must be added that, by many of his students, his orthodox formulas were parroted, his favorite quotations requoted, his attitudes mimed. For this superficial imitation of a master, however, Harvard alone could furnish sufficient parallels, most notably in Kittredge. But men's normal growth in virtue and wisdom comes, I think, from the imitation of their heroes; their spiritual history is the history of their friendships and their admirations. So feeble an originality as not to survive pupillage seems scarcely worth preservation.

It may seem strange that, so admiring Babbitt, I made no calls upon him at his office, never sought a personal relationship with him. It was my very admiration for Babbitt which deterred me. I felt I had no right to take up the time of a man so learned and so wise, to keep him from his greatly important writing. Furthermore, I was deriving such richness from his lectures and from trying to read all the great authors he cited with respect that I felt no need for more.

In later years, I learned that Babbitt, isolated among his colleagues, was a lonely man who would have appreciated calls from a sympathetic, admiring young man, even would have invited him for walks. Yet perhaps I might still have drawn back, feeling, rightly, that the disproportion in mental vigor between master and disciple might have overpowered me. Perhaps I feared assenting, or seeming to assent, when I didn't: I suffered in my youth from pain at dissenting openly from older men whom I respected, and then from pangs of conscience that I had suppressed my dissent.

My course with Babbitt had one consequence almost comic. Although the course was in Rousseau and Romanticism, I ended it without reading anything by Rousseau. We students were given a long reading list to select from, and doubtless Rousseau's principal works were on it; but so were the *Analects* of Confucius and the *Dhammapada* of Buddha and the *Ethics* of Aristotle. As Babbitt had made it so clear that Rousseau was dubious of character and not only mistaken but pernicious in his doctrines, I decided that it was a waste of time to read him; so I turned my attention to Confucius, Buddha, Aristotle, and whatever else was referred to as sound, salutary and "central."

Babbitt was, to be sure, not only a professor of French but of comparative literature, which, I would later understand, warranted his dealing with all European literatures, unmindful of national boundaries; but that was a concept and even term I did not then comprehend. However, he far exceeded and transcended even comparative literature: one might say simply that he was a comparativist. He compared East and West, civilizations, philosophies, and religions, tracing continuities and making contrasts, richly—and with much wry humor and satire—opposing the wisdom of the ages to the grotesque and pathetic eccentricities and aberrations of the present.

Although I was something of an aesthete as well as a Yankee moralist, I was not disturbed by the absence of the aesthetic in Babbitt's makeup: I much preferred him to the aesthetically impressionistic (as well as learned) Lowes. I saw in Babbitt a philosopher, a life philosopher, who did what most of the academic philosophers of the time did not—concerned himself with the whole spectrum of central human values, most notably religion, ethics, and politics.

From Babbitt I derived something more, which has stayed with me, steadying and nerving me: the sense that a professor need not, indeed should not, be a mere historian or compiler of opinions and views of other men; that he should be a man as well as a scholar, which means that he must judge and evaluate and take positions, and not only in his specialty. He must have the "courage to be." Whenever I have weakly abnegated this responsibility, I have felt the example of Babbitt, both in his person and in his books, as a censure and a spur.

After my year at Harvard, I taught as an instructor for two years at the University of Minnesota, a post for which I was chosen, it pleases me to recall, by Joseph Warren Beach, who visited Harvard to inspect candidates for instructorships. During those two years of teaching, I saved up enough money to put myself through two further years of graduate study.

I did not return to Harvard. The general influence of Babbitt was such as to discourage his disciples from taking a doctorate at all, at least at Harvard, on the ground that the emphasis there was all on scholarly research, that criticism was not within the permissible scope. He and his ally, Paul Elmer More, who was later my friend, had both declined to narrow their studies to achieve the doctorate; and there was always open to young men of self-definition, and willing to work, the alternative of fitting themselves for an academic post and subsequent promotion by writing and publishing.

I have felt at times mildly conscience stricken that I did not, at twenty-four, take that line; but at that age I lacked requisite self-definition, did not yet see myself as a writer and a critic; nor did I rebel at the thought of more graduate study. I had enough faith in myself to think I could comply with the requirements of my teachers without distortion of myself or undue resentment of them.

I had, however, no desire to return to Harvard, feeling that, having studied with all its famous men, and having had one great teacher and master, Babbitt, I had had the good of Harvard. Yale I probably ruled out because I had no desire to follow in Benny's footsteps. Columbia and Johns Hopkins and Chicago I never considered. That left Princeton. I knew no Princeton graduates; and I no more knew, even by name, the full professors, the "eminencies," than I did when I set out for Harvard. All I did know was from hearsay, that it had a Graduate College modeled, architecturally and in tone, on Oxford, and that the system was less rigorously philological—and therefore presumably more humanistic—than that of Harvard.

Two embarrassments attended my entrance into the Graduate College, both due to my naïveté and my absence of any older friends, especially ones connected with Princeton, duly to advise me. I had, throughout my early years, the conception that scholarships were not based on intellectual merit but on poverty: so I did not ask for what I viewed as financial aid either at Wesleyan or at Princeton. I applied for entrance to the Graduate School, but did not realize, till I had been in residence for a few months, that the rank and file of graduate students there were all Procter Fellows, their tuition and living expenses all paid by the named patron. My second disappointment, probably due to my not having applied in time, was my failure to get living quarters in the neo-Gothic Graduate College itself. For my first year I was housed in a rented annex, a kind of rooming house for a few beginning graduate students and a bachelor assistant professor of engineering. These were but the most conspicuous ways in which I felt myself marked as an outsider.

Despite my lack of advance knowledge and advice and letters of recommendation, I could not have chosen, for my own purposes, better than I did; and, even in my first year, when I did not live at the College but only ate there, I was moderately happy.

The College was a ten or fifteen minute walk from the campus and thus, distinct and separate from the undergraduates (just as Princeton, unlike Harvard, had no classes mixing undergraduates and graduates). The building was of stone; its windows—most of them, romantically, casements—opened out on a closely cropped English-like lawn or onto Dean West's rose garden. For breakfast and lunch, there were provided dark-paneled, low-studded Tudor rooms. Dinner was served in the Great Hall, marble paved, and provided with an organ gallery over its entrance and a grandiose stained glass window at the farther end. The black-gowned students filed into dinner led by the proctor, a silver-haired bachelor who pronounced the grace in Latin.

This society of young American scholars was hierarchic. At the top, the supreme snobs were the fine arts men, especially the archaeologists and medievalists. Next, *magno intervallo*, came the literary folk. The physical scientists, a few excepted, drew up the rear. In addition to the American hierarchy, there were—harder to place, as foreigners must ever be—the British and European Fellows: two Englishmen, one from Oxford and one from Cambridge; a Frenchman; a Scandinavian; and a Russian. These British and Continental young men, whatever their academic specialty, excelled their American equivalents in general culture; they were my natural friends. Among them I recall a Russian chemist, and a British classicist, and the vivacious Frenchman, Jean Catel, who amazed and shocked Princeton's English professors by coming to study, and to write a book upon, that American barbarian, Walt Whitman.

All the graduates were taught in seminars, seldom exceeding six or seven members. During my first year, I had a seminar in the Gothic tongue with J. Duncan Spaeth, a hearty character who was also the only teacher of American literature but chiefly known as the rowing coach. With Charles Kennedy, not an exciting full professor, I had my second course in Old English, its blessing being that I had the opportunity to study and to write my term paper on Cynewulf's *Christ*, a devout and richly ornate poem, full of schemes and tropes—a poem which converted me to the view that Old English had a literature but left me pained that its professors— teaching it purely as a linguistic discipline—did not see it as art.

It was apparently improper at Princeton for the professors offering seminars to make any preparation for them: their comments were casual *obiter dicta*. This was most noticeably the case with the locally venerated Professor Parrott, who taught Elizabethan drama. British and tweedy in style, he rarely moved his pipe from his mouth as he extemporized and commented. He did not favor reasons and judicial criticism; but his critical laxity allowed me to write a term paper according to my own convictions. As a Latinist and Babbittian humanist, I naturally viewed most of the dramatists to whom the seminar was devoted, from which we had to chose one writer for a long term paper, as "unsound"; but, happily, our repertory included Ben Jonson, classicist both as playwright and critic; and so I had my appropriate man.

Much my favorite of the Princeton professors was Robert Wilbur Root, with whom I had, in 1924–25, a seminar, and who the next year directed my doctoral dissertation. Root was a scholar with two fields, Chaucer and the eighteenth century, both of which had relevance to Root's roots, for, like his close friend,

Tinker of Yale, he was a high Anglican and ever careful of his dress, and his speech. He was also an excellent drillmaster of graduate students, a teacher of research methods, resourceful in devices and projects, relentless and just in condemning alike factual inaccuracy and loose thinking on the part of his students. Like Tinker and like their great teacher at Yale, Albert S. Cook, Root was also, as I recognized, a kind of proto–New Humanist. On the subject of New Humanism, imbued with which at Harvard I came to Princeton, Root never spoke out; but I felt his silent sympathy, qualified though it was by his shrinking from the crude enthusiasm of both Babbitt and his young disciple.

Root's seminar was devoted to Swift and Pope. After exercises in both, we ended with term papers, and I chose for mine the topic of Pope's literary criticism. Pope's poetry I had been interested in at least since my early twenties, though I first met with it in my sophomore year at Wesleyan. I was attracted by the precision of its form and its subtle variations within limits. It also felt its continuity with the Roman authors, especially Horace, whom I had studied at Wesleyan. I vaguely perceived also some analogy between Pope's poetry and Mozart's music. Perhaps in Pope Mozart's delicacy was combined with the commonsense humanism of Handel.

Out of my term paper and Root's seminar, my dissertation, *Pope as Literary Critic*, developed. I don't remember whether Mr. Root suggested it to me, or I to him. In any case, I was surprised and delighted at the concord. Because of the tradition passed on from graduate student to graduate student, I had assumed that I would not be free to choose my subject, to write on something which would interest me; indeed, that any subject I thus proposed would be ruled out as not providing sufficient intellectual (i.e., moral) discipline: writing a dissertation was, by definition, something to be done against the grain.

The traditional belief may have some foundation. There have been, I understand, professors who, with some large scheme in mind for themselves, have used their students to do, by way of directed dissertations, much of their spadework, providing the specificities upon which the more mature or ambitious teacher can generalize. And, too, many, perhaps most, students have no strongly marked interests or tastes: they request to be set a topic, and might just as well, for purposes of intellectual economy, be assigned one in the line of the director's own interests, studies, and plans for future writing. But my case, while exemplary, is not, I suppose, markedly unusual. I had a strong interest; I had chosen an excellent subject; my director already had a liking for Pope. So my proposal was accepted; I was invited to do what I wanted to do.

Mr. Root was the sole reader and judge of my dissertation while it was in progress. But after he had accepted it, it was passed on to the second reader, Morris Croll, who invited me to his home for an hour's gentle and encouraging conference. Mr. Croll was, without question, the one genius in the Princeton English department, which ran to urbane gentlemen, intellectually of a high-class mediocrity. I deeply regret that I never had a course with him (whose brilliant discourse prefaced to *Euphues* I discovered and read at Princeton). Root, Parrott, Osgood, and Gerould, who, officially or unofficially, advised graduate students with whom to study, discriminated against Harper, the Wordsworthian, and Croll, on grounds never stated. They were presumably too creative or too critical, certainly not "correct"and "sound"enough. But I did have my fragile connection with Croll, and, not too long after I left Princeton, became an admiring reader of his distinguished, even elegant, work on stylistics.

The dissertation was composed under the most agreeable circumstances. I was not married, hence, not a parent; I was not a part-time teacher, and hence divided between educating myself and trying to educate others. My final year at Princeton, 1925–26, was entirely mine, to be spent on the making of a book.

That year I lived in the Graduate College, designed by the great neo-Medievalist Cram. Like its other inhabitants, I had sole occupancy of a small paneled study with an adjoining smaller bedroom—the study lighted by casement windows which opened on some kind of view. Breakfast and lunch were served in the Tudor paneled rooms; dinners in the stone-paved dining hall. At our meals we were served by young waiters of recent importation from Europe. There was a spacious Common Room.

After a leisurely breakfast at eight, I went to the Common Room and played the piano for an hour—generally four-hand music performed with a fellow student. I worked in my study from ten to twelve: had lunch, took a nap; worked an hour more. Before dinner, I went, generally with a friend, for a long walk along the canal which led from Princeton to Trenton, or through the gardens of the nearby Pyne estate. After dinner, I often attended a concert or a lecture. I had time, too, for miscellaneous reading—chiefly theology.

How did I write? It was not real writing, alas; hence I prefer to speak, in this case, rather of composing or making a book. It was mostly what Benny used to call "scissors and paste" work. That is, under Dr. Root's training, I had learned how to take 3 × 5 cards, copy out on them all the passages from Pope's works and those of his commentators on a topic (e.g., Pope's reading in earlier English literature); next, to spread out my cards, to arrange and rearrange them till they made the best order, logical or chronological; then to paste my quotations together by writing, really writing, some transitions between them. These transitions consisted largely in paraphrases, in my own uneven style, of what had better been said in the preceding or succeeding quotation. Then the chapter would end, as it had begun, with a paragraph of my own—at least, that is, one not quoted but written by me.

When I composed my first book, I was following orthodox scholarly procedure. I was to be a compiler, not the writer of a really independent critical monograph. Sometimes, not being by nature a compiler, I struck out a good bold sentence of my own. In the *Pope* book there are a few sentences which sound like those of a real writer and even like myself.

This last year at Princeton was indeed idyllic. I had passed the language tests in French and German; I had passed the three-day general written examination; I had completed the requisite number of seminars. I no longer had to visit the campus except to bring, more or less once a month, a chapter of my book to Mr. Root, or to draw books from the university library. Otherwise, my day was my own; and the writing of the dissertation, which some students seem to dread or find boring, I found a constant pleasure—a steady, quiet, daily task which offered all manner of unexpected discoveries, insights, and perspectives. For a prime example, since Pope's practical criticism was chiefly exercised on the poets of the period just before his own, it was through his critical comments on Crashaw that I was introduced to both that poet on whom I later wrote, and to metaphysical and baroque poetry in general.

Nor was my reading, during that year, limited to my topic. There were two extraordinarily rich theological libraries at hand— one belonging to the university, and one to the nearby Presbyterian seminary—the latter, curiously as I thought, not limited, either in books or periodicals, to the Protestant tradition: it abounded in Catholic works like Baron von Hugel's *The Mystical Element in Religion* and Pourrat's *La Spiritualité chrétienne*. I made generous use of the library; and I read widely in philosophy and theology as well as literature.

My daily work gave me happiness. So did the general leisurely atmosphere of Princeton and its Graduate College. And I made, my second year, two special friends—one, Henry Grubbs, who had been an undergraduate at Princeton and now was a Procter Fellow in French, specializing in the seventeenth century, a "civilized" man indeed, with whom I later traveled in the south of France; the other Edmund Halsey, then a freshman, but one above the usual age and learned in Anglican and Catholic theology, whom I met by chance one day at church. These were both excellent walking companions, and both had much to teach me.

The attitude toward me of my sponsor, Professor Root, became increasingly friendly. I was still socially too incorrect for him to be comfortable with me, or for him to take me in hand and really bring me up, as he, who was both a high Anglican and an admirer and editor of Lord Chesterfield, could, to my profit, have done; but he was increasingly surprised and impressed by my energy and ambition and my intellectual insight, in evidence of which he was ready to give me a year's appointment as Princeton instructor for the following year. I have much to thank Mr. Root for: he really taught me scholarly method. After Babbitt—and an excellent supplement and correction to Babbitt, he was the professor from whom I most learned.

Unlike some students, I did not resent graduate school or my professors. Only Babbitt and Root did I truly admire; to the rest and their requirements, I felt superior; but, I reasoned, if I am not able to perform to their satisfaction the academic exercises they set, I am not the superior young man I estimate myself to be: as a would-be critic and humanist, I must "transcend by including" the humbler offices of scholarship. In general, I combined, with much external docility to my official teachers, a good deal of self-assurance—perhaps even arrogance. As a Christian humanist, I knew what I believed and what I stood for.

While I was a graduate student, I was already, from 1923 on, the dean of St. Peter's School of Liberal and Humane Studies, which met for two weeks each summer at Hebron, Connecticut. With my cofounder, Benny Bissell, then a young university instructor, we had founded an institution which, though, it was visible only for a summer fortnight, we conceived of as Platonically ever in existence. This chiefly invisible and yet briefly realized institution, and our importance as its founders and directors, sustained us both during years when, from a public point of view, our status was humble.

5

St. Peter's School: An Experiment in Community

In the summer of 1921, my Wesleyan friend, Benny, returned to Hebron, Connecticut, to visit remote relatives who lived outside the village and his mother's friend, Miss Caroline Kellogg, who had inherited late in life an old, square, white house, facing the village green. Benny had spent his childhood in Hebron, but his parents had moved to the city of Hartford, and there, not long after their removal, died.

Coming back for the first time, at least in his adult life, to Hebron, he was charmed by the village, almost unaltered since his childhood—still rural and isolated, left behind by modern progress. The telephone had made its appearance, but there was no running water—hence no bathrooms, only the old backhouses or privies; and there was no electricity—hence the unpaved streets were unlighted. In the preceding century, a fire had burned down the old pre–Civil War houses on one side of the village green and burned down the old white meetinghouse of the Congregational church, till well after the Revolution the established church or the "standing order," as it was called, the tax-supported religious sect; but the rest of the village was untouched, and there was still the old red brick church dedicated to St. Peter, and just endowment enough still to keep a resident rector—an eccentric bachelor or an elderly man—serving his last parish before he retired: such a latter was the incumbent in 1921 and long after. Prosperous before the Civil War, the church had now shrunk to a pair of families—one, the daughter and son-in-law of a former rector, who now lived eight or ten miles away, and one, the only resident family, the Pendletons, who lived just across the street from Benny's old home, and only a few doors from the church.

The following summer, Benny, then the houseguest of Miss Kellogg, invited me to visit him for a week, which I did. Our hostess, who served as village librarian and organist of St. Peter's Church, was an eccentric, witty, sharp-tongued elderly woman. She and I did not hit it off very well. During that first visit, I commented on the Victorian stained glass windows which to my taste so marred the otherwise impeccable St. Peter's, applying to them the epithet "cheap." "Indeed, they are not cheap," my hostess replied, "some of them were given by my relatives; and they were expensive." Later I came to appreciate these windows as period pieces; meanwhile I had received a needed lesson in tact and caution.

The two chief pleasures of that shared first week were found in the church and in the Pendleton family.

Though the church was unused except for one service on Sunday morning, it was always open. We began to hold daily morning and evening prayer for ourselves, Benny reading the two scripture lessons and the prayers, and I playing the opening and closing hymns on the small reed organ which stood by the lectern. Occasionally, the older Pendleton sisters attended.

The Pendletons' father had passed his life as the village physician, but had retained, from his college years at Williams, his fondness for the classics: his big Greek dictionary still stood beside the medical books in his office. He was also the local historian, and contributed a chronicle to the Hebron bicentennial of 1910, for which his daughter Susan, who inherited his interest in local lore, contributed the ode.

When Benny and I came to know Hebron, father and mother were both dead; the only son practiced medicine in the nearby town of Colchester. Father and mother had both been Congregationalists and Republicans, and such remained their son and married daughter, Mrs. Lord, still living in Hebron. But, at some time, the other three daughters, who lived on in their parents' house, had become—what in Hebron, and in Connecticut generally, went together—both Episcopalians and Democrats. The eldest sister— Miss Pendleton, as she would have been called in Jane Austen's England; Clarissa, as she had been named; Miss Clara, as we called her—had for some years left Hebron and practiced as a nurse. Miss Susan—Susie, as she was locally known—had gone to normal school and taught school for a few years, but, finding the children made her nervous, she returned home and made a modest income by acting as local correspondent for the daily newspapers in the nearby cities of Middletown, Hartford, and South Manchester. She also wrote poems good enough to appear in the little magazines of the 1920s and in at least one anthology. The third sister, Mrs. Anne Gilbert, who had been married, had divorced her husband, and had returned home with her one child, a daughter, was the plainest and most practical of the sisters; and, appropriately, she earned a modest sum as town clerk of Hebron.

The three sisters, all in their fifties when I first knew them, were very different in type. Miss Clara, who must have been the belle of the family, and still retained autumnal beauty, was also the saint. Untheological, she was a natural mystic, who had for a time lived in an Anglo-Catholic city parish, had read some theological books, was unostentatiously devout, but most of all was eminent, and cherished, and reverenced for her tenderness, her sympathy for the poor, ill, or eccentric, her simple loving-kindness. It is strange that she had never married: she had nothing repressed about her; yet she seemed fulfilled, like a nun. Perhaps she had renounced a possible marriage; there was about her a quiet note of transcendent renunciation.

I loved Miss Clara; but my favorite was Miss Susan, the individualist among them—vivid, strong, and impetuous of spirit, full of vivacity and wit and a snappy temper, as well as moody and intensely Romantic. Not only the village poetess and historian, she was also the speculative mind of the village. On the subject of religion, she had neither Clara's simple piety nor the belligerent skepticism of the village organist and librarian. Miss Kellogg was reputed once to have encountered the rector on his placid way to the post office and confronted him with the question, "What and where is God?" to which he replied confusedly that he couldn't give her an immediate answer but would go home and look it up in his books. Miss Susan, however, entertained a proper intuition that orthodox and Catholic religion raised the really deep philosophical questions about the meaning of values, though one need not accept its dogmas as more than symbols or starting points for inquiry.

Plain and practical Ann, or Annie, Gilbert—Benny delighted in referring to all these ladies by the youthful and village versions of their names—was not one to delight me or one who could especially approve of me; but the Pendleton sisters, strongly individuated as they were, presented a united front to the world; and her sisters, Clara and Susan, believed in me—and Benny came of an old Hebron family; and her daughter, Helen, was interested in "the boys" and might marry one of them.

Daughter Helen, who taught children and was away from home except in the summers, was dainty and pretty; dressed and talked in a style considerably younger than her presumed age, never known, but slightly older than mine. Like her aunt Susan, whose rival in a way she was, she was a practicing and, in little magazines, a publishing poet—a poet in a style several generations later than that of her aunt—a writer in free and rather wispy verse. About the relative merits of the two poets, judgment of critics, local and other, differed; I preferred the rugged and rather rustic but intense poetry of Miss Susan.

A remarkable family: and Benny and I were more or less, from our first summer in Hebron, adopted into it. Without the Pendletons, their local position, and their house, always open to us, there could not have taken place what did.

What did was the idea which grew in Benny's head and mine, almost in unison, of founding in Hebron a community, a summer gathering of friends sharing our interests in religion and culture. Our own week, framed by daily morning and evening prayer in the historic parish church of St. Peter's, was to be developed by filling that ecclesiastical framework with appropriate lectures and "conversations" (this word I use in the sense that Bronson Alcott and Margaret Fuller used it; the Platonic word *dialogues* might also have served).

The beginning of such an enterprise would not have been possible without enlisting if not the enthusiastic support at least the tolerance and legal permission of the rector of St. Peter's, the Reverend Theodore Martin, a handsome, white-haired old man, now serving his last parish before retirement. He was a priest of moderate intelligence—not a scholar or a thinker, rather tactless, but city bred and educated at the Choir School of Trinity Church, New York. He was married to an at once beautiful and sensible woman, without any special religious feelings, who had all her life done her best to cover up her husband's mistakes and treat him with public respect. She had, when I knew her, the compensation of a hobby—a taste for New England antiques, which she bought judiciously and restored with a craftsman's skill.

"Father" Martin was a Low Churchman, and perhaps properly suspicious of Benny and me as High Church and conspiratorially plotting (after the fashion of Anglo-Catholics) some ritualistic damage to Hebron. Village fear rumored that we intended to hand over St. Peter's, Hebron, to the pope, who also had a St. Peter's, in Rome. This suspicion was not easily allayed. But we had two innocent bribes to offer, which won the rector over. The first was our recognition of his fine baritone voice, fine alike in reading and in singing. From the formal beginning of the school, in the summer of 1923, till the end, the rector conducted our daily services; and, on Sundays, during the school, he sang all the priest's part in Merbecke's Elizabethan setting of the Communion service, and sang them well. By feeding his musical vanity, we secured his liturgical compliance. Then, as the school continued on, through the summer of 1931—nine years in all, the rector found also that his own status, locally and in the diocese, had been elevated; and, among the annual favorable accounts of the school sent in to the *Connecticut Churchman,* the official monthly magazine of the Diocese of Connecticut, some were from his pen.

With the rector's permission secured and the Pendletons' backing, at least a modest success was assured. Miss Susan became the chairwoman of our trustees, a purely nominal office; Mrs. Gilbert our bursar (or treasurer), a minimal duty, since the lecturers were unpaid; and Helen became our secretary, which amounted to chairwoman in care of social events. The letter writing about the school, which went on, importantly, all through the year, was conducted by Benny and me, and was chiefly between us.

There were practical arrangements to be made, but they proved simple. Since the village public library was open but two afternoons a week, our lectures, morning affairs, were held there, librarian Kellogg, Benny's old friend and regular summer hostess, commonly present as an auditor. Out-of-town lecturers and students were lodged in private houses; and we all took our meals in common at what we called the "Refectory," a house which had in earlier times been the village inn and tavern. It was now owned by Mrs. Gertrude Hough, a kind, motherly Congregationalist, who still boarded whatever strangers turned up in town; and she treated us to simple country fare, running heavily to starchy foods—potato, bread, and layer cake, but otherwise wholesome; our table waited on by her daughters. The evening parties were held at the Pendletons' or Miss Kellogg's or Mrs. Martin's.

Our precedents for the school were Little Gidding and Bronson Alcott's Concord School of Philosophy; our intention, to give corporate form to Christian humanism, as represented by the powerful influences of Irving Babbitt, my teacher at Harvard, and Albert

S. Cook, Benny's at Yale. What we designed was conceived of, and became, an intellectual community.

Always the thought was of a community in permanent existence. We, who made ourselves, as is the right of founders, president and dean of St. Peter's, conceived, fancifully, of an enterprise which should gradually become the central activity of Hebron—an enterprise including a kind of lay monastery (like Little Gidding), a school for boys, a publishing house—designed both for propaganda and for the promotion of hand printing. Perhaps there would even be shops for handmade furniture and fabrics after the example of William Morris and Eric Gill. These ambitious plans never had any even modest realization.

There was a theoretical view of the school which, because it was theoretical, could not be refuted; such a view we, the founders, took with intense earnestness. Though our community was visibly in existence for only a fortnight each summer, we refused to think of it, or permit others to call it, a summer school or summer conference. Such schools, of course, were already widely and usefully in operation; but we did not identify our community with them. St. Peter's was conceived of as always in existence in the Platonic World of Ideas.

Because it was a community and not a school in the modern sense, it had an analogy to the army of the kingdom of Oz: it was almost an army composed of officers. The school, said, proudly, an early prospectus, "confers no degrees, gives no credits, and offers no courses in utilitarian subjects." The members of the community ranged from college juniors and seniors to men and women of seventy and eighty. Perhaps half of them were Hebron residents—the "cultivated" ones—including the rector and the village librarian; half were younger people of both sexes. The lecturers were imported, but not paid. Since there were at least as many lecturers as nonlecturing students, I, in my function of dean, early made a rule, one worth emulation, that each of the lecturers must attend the lectures given by others. The immediate motive of the rule was doubtless practical, to assure each of us who lectured an audience: but I could, and did, theoretically defend it on the ground of the school's liberal and humanistic character. "St. Peter's people" were not assembled as specialists, but as members of a cultural community.

The school had a double character. It belonged to the world of essence and to the world of existence. Like any institution, it belonged to history as well as to theory. The residents of Hebron saw it chiefly as history—as persons and events, as amusement or outrage. Those not natives, especially the president and the dean, were aware always of the mixture—sometimes grotesque, often, at some level, comic—of the ideal and the actual.

Because the school existed in time and space, as well as in eternity and ubiquity, it can be described only by taking now one aspect and then the other. First come place and period.

The village of Hebron goes back into the eighteenth century; and the doctrinal oppositions, political and ecclesiastical, of the century were still strong. Connecticut never underwent the Harvard-disseminated Unitarian movement which reached its crisis about 1830. Yale, the university of Edwards, Dwight, and Bellamy—held to the Calvinist persuasion; but a minority of Yale men like Seabury (first American bishop, after the Revolution) and Johnson (first president of King's College, later Columbia) espoused episcopacy. In Hebron as in most Connecticut towns and villages, the choice was between the Congregational church (often called the "Orthodox") and the Episcopal.

In 1922, when I first visited Hebron, it was a decadent village "behind the times" in a fashion unknown to the eastern part of Massachusetts familiar to me. It was difficult even to reach. A branch line landed the traveler at a small railroad station three miles out of town, and from there he paid to ride into Hebron with the generally intoxicated mailman.

In 1922, and during most of the school's existence, Hebron had no modern conveniences. The nonresident members of the school, who came chiefly from New York or Boston, were carried into another world: the surprise, an insight into history, being that civilization was possible without any of these supposed American necessities. The older—and resident—members of the school walked home from evening parties and concerts, elegantly dressed, but carrying lanterns—as used to do the ladies of Cranford. President Bissell and Dean Warren quickly turned these Hebron backwardnesses to doctrinal account; they tested whether prospective members were really worthy of being St. Peter's people, which involved their being able to distinguish between culture and "modern improvements." The test worked out to our satisfaction.

The center of the school was the Episcopal church, St. Peter's, from which the school took its name. The parish, as its rector, Mr. Martin, once casually remarked in an anniversary sermon, had "continued to dwindle"—for the last forty of fifty years. But whatever the state of the congregations, the fine old church remained.

And the historic parish went back to the eighteenth century, when "Connecticut churchmanship"—orthodox and catholic but unritualistic—took its rise.

One of the first rectors of St. Peter's was the Reverend Samuel Peters, Hebron-born but a Tory and a High Churchman. Run out of the village at the time of the Revolution, he went to England and there published a book, the *General History of Connecticut*, "to be read with caution" for its occasional fictions, and its strong anti-Puritan bias, but both a delightful satire of the Puritans and a spirited presentation of the loyalist position. Behind the church, in St. Peter's churchyard, Dr. Peters is commemorated by a high-soaring soi-disant Gothic monument.

The church I knew, built in 1810, was intended by its architect to be Venetian Gothic, but the wooden pinnacles adorning facade and tower proved unequal to New England storms; and, except for the unusual position of the belfry tower, behind the chancel, St. Peter's had come to look like a Georgian church, built of sound brick—not in the least the kind of cottage shingle Gothic easily recognizable in so many New England villages as the Episcopal chapel.

Parish churches, like other buildings, are often architecturally and otherwise helped by lack of funds. And St. Peter's had enjoyed this blessing. The square pews, with doors, still remained. The organ, built by Johnson of Westfield, Massachusetts, during the good old days of sound diapason and reed construction, in 1860, had remained unimproved by orchestral imitations and tremolos; and it remained where organs should remain, in a gallery over the west entrance.

Behind the church was the churchyard, which, after the exhaustion of the old Anglican and Congregational graveyards, had come to serve the dead of the whole village. It was just what a graveyard should be; and Benny and I and other St. Peter's people often strolled through it in the postsupper twilight. The dead were not segregated from the living—not tactfully or cheerfully forgotten—for the yard sloped down a gentle incline from the chancel end of the church. On one side of it was a cow pasture and cows; and at its lower end there was the prospect of forest-covered hills. Farmers cut the grass of the graveyard when the haying was over; but the irregular grass did not matter, any more than the variety— period or personal—of the monuments: an obelisk out of the native red sandstone; a Carrara marble angel with arm and finger pointing heavenward; a huge boulder of fieldstone over the grave of Dr. Cyrus Pendleton, the last "family doctor" to live in the village.

The visible school, which met for two weeks each summer, for nine years, was assembled in just the right way.

The small fee, coming annually from twenty or thirty persons, paid only for what a larger kind of enterprise would call incidentals: it paid the wage of the organ blower (whatever local boy was strong enough to pump "full organ" yet not strong or old enough to be gainfully employed); it paid for the ice cream served at parties. Most important, it paid for the annual prospectus, which was a matter of serious concern to the president and the dean. Though these prospectuses did announce the courses and lectures for the coming summer, its chief function was doctrinal. Statements worded as carefully as a platform or creed were supplemented by bibliographies documenting the intellectual position of the school.

Yet, not more than a college catalog, was the prospectus the means of assembling the school. During the school's existence, Benny and I were young instructors at sundry universities. But wherever we taught—at Indiana, California, Boston—we passed rigorous scrutiny upon our colleagues and our pupils, the question being ever, "Are these worthy of being St. Peter's people?" It was not the school or its principles which were on trial, nor was the prospectus intended as an advertisement to all and sundry. St. Peter's School was to be an Arnoldian "saving remnant," to which only the "elect," and selected, received the honor of admission.

This was the principle. In practice, the school, composed naturally, of "the friends of the friends," admitted members neither easy to square with its platform nor easy to adjust to the mores of a New England village.

For example, President Bissell had formed—in Indiana—a personal friendship with an extraordinarily learned comparativist and folklorist, Dr. Alexander Krappe, whose books, written in English, French, or German, are masterly, but who, on grounds biographically intelligible, was uncouth in person and dress, and arrogant and brash, in the Menckenian style. He was crudely satirical of the Christian religion as well as of the United States. Religion was "taking out fire insurance." The national flag was "the Star Spangled Banana." The great American newspaper was the New York "Behind the Times."

Lecturing, in the presence of the elderly rector and the no less elderly and more acerb village librarian, on the migration of folk myths, the great scholar made a point of using, as his illustrative motif, the copulation of serpents. Yet even that proved less offensive, doubtless because less intelligible, than the same scholar's loud-lunged reference to the Hough daughters, who waited upon the refectory table, as "peasants." The imputation was promptly resented by the local Congregationalists; and Dr. Krappe had to be removed to solitary meals—which he professed much to prefer—at the other end of Hebron.

Whatever else it is, a Connecticut village is the opposite of an assembly line. As the Boston poet, Jack Wheelwright, used to say, every New Englander instinctively replies "No"—even before he hears a question or an invitation. Village people are all individuals, characters, each of whom must be reckoned with, argued with, separately. They will not be "beholden" to any one; and they feel free at any time to alter their vote.

The villagers were independents but, then, so were the younger school people who came from New York and Boston. It was the liability, as well as the special advantage, of the school that it was composed chiefly of "geniuses"—as incapable of ready concession or tact as the villagers. Even Dr. Krappe was a genius as well as scholar; but almost all St. Peter's people were what would then have been called temperamental. Some were poets; some violinists or pianists; all were "gifted."

It was my chief function as dean to adjust the school to the village Congregationalists and Republicans and then to adjust the school geniuses to one another. I certainly possessed no inborn tact: I was, to my own view, some kind of genius myself; and I certainly abounded in principles and doctrines on all subjects. But the cause of the school was precious to me—not least the unavowed, perhaps unconsciously held, cause of a community of independents, united not by forcible authority but by understanding and love. So I found myself engaged not only in interpreting doctrine to people but in interpreting one person, one soul, to another; and this was most of all valuable to me, who so needed to develop empathy and sympathy, and even common sense.

The schedule of the school was strenuous. After the communal breakfast at eight, St. Peter's bell rang out for nine o'clock matins or, on Wednesday and Friday, for sung litany. Then followed three hours of lectures, each ordinarily concluding with discussion.

The first session offered courses in Aeschylus, Dante, and the development of the mediaeval short story; the second, studies in the Latin hymns, the psychology of religion, Elizabethan tragedy, Pater, and the European folksong; the third, Church history, seventeenth-century English poetry, the poetry of Pope, the history of baroque music.

In 1930, with the eighth session, the founders drew up a program synoptic but devoted to a single historic period, the eighteenth century, each lecturer addressing himself to topics in his own world of discourse, worlds comprising theology, English and American literature, economic theory, music, history, and historiography.

At one o'clock midday dinner was ready. There followed two hours unscheduled, during which some of our company rested and some, chiefly the youngest, drove to a nearby lake for swimming.

At four, the community reassembled on the porch of the Pendleton house for a discussion conducted, but by no means dominated, by Professor Hite of Cambridge, our venerable philosopher. After the fashion of forums, there was a literal question box, into which any sufficiently broad query, whether submitted by old skeptics or young enthusiasts, might find entrance. Questions were likely to be of the Socratic order. "What is beauty?" "What is truth?" "What is virtue?" Mr. Hite, a philosopher by temper of mind as well as profession, was often content to round off a many-sided controversy by saying, "This will show you all how complex truth is."

On one occasion, when the Rt. Reverend E. Campion Acheson, the bishop of Connecticut, unaccustomed to being contradicted, visited the school and attended the "Question Box," he took it upon himself to answer, with the authority of an apostolic prelate, one of the questions, and did so not alone as expounding the catechism to children but as himself still one who thought as a child. Interrogated or set right by our mild-voiced philosopher, the bishop grew purple with an irritation felt by St. Peter's people not to be wholly spiritual.

At quarter of five, St. Peter's bell began to ring for evensong. For some, perhaps many of us, and certainly for me, evensong was the peaceful center of the day. By no means all of St. Peter's people were Episcopalians. They included even a local Congregationalist young woman, of whom the rector of Hebron once said—not humorously but to reassure—"Clarissa is a Congregationalist . . . but she is a *good* girl!" And there were some out-of-town students, including two or three young Jews, who professed no religion. But these made no objection to our rule of regular attendance. Evensong was, for all, a time of meditation. It admitted no doctrinal, still less dogmatic, utterances from the pulpit, nor sermon or homily. The lessons and collects were well read; the Canticles and the Psalms appointed for the day were sung to the Gregorian tones. The hymns had to be, and were, at once theologically, literarily, and musically sound. Soundness in church music was, indeed, one of the school's concerns. Most of its male members were, in varying degrees of skill, musicians, as was also, of course, the rector. The church music—precisely because, for all the males of the school, it involved first principles—was a matter of considerable tension. The rector's taste, generational, properly but troublesomely, was for the bright, rapid, allegretto Anglican hymn tunes of the nineteenth century, the tunes, chromatically harmonized, of Dykes and Barnby; while Benny and I, young zealots, schooled on the *English Hymnal*, wished to expel almost the whole nineteenth-century hymnody in favor of plainsong melodies, German chorales, Geneva psalm tunes, and old English, Irish, Scotch, or Welsh folksongs. Following the tenets laid down by Robert Bridges and his disciples, I, who played St. Peter's organ, insisted that all of the congregation sing the melody, and held myself ready to transpose the tune to a gamut within the range of all. The rector, however, wanted to sing the bass part of the written harmony—not, like men uneducated in music, the tune. Our whole hymnodic fare was repellent to him: he groaned often, to Benny and me, "You boys like only doleful tunes in the minor keys!"

The musicological conflict between the two ends of the church had an amusing practical consequence. Whoever would first reach the church and post the numbers on the hymn board could prescribe the taste of the service. But the rector was in the main defeated by the very substitution, during the school, of *English Hymnals*, borrowed from the Berkeley Divinity School at Middletown, books almost devoid of "cheerful tunes," for the good old Hutchins hymnal used all the rest of the year.

The rectory and the house of the Pendletons, and occasionally other houses, were open to us for social gatherings; and every evening the school had some divertissement: sometimes a card party, at which some played bridge while the conservatives, of whom I was one, made a point of simple whist.

Sometimes there was square dancing, the only mode of dancing which the school held to be "sound." At one gathering, both the rector and the professor of philosophy, two clergymen in clerical black, danced the Virginia reel with the eldest gentlewomen present—the effect being one of stately ritual and historic continuity. It gave us members of the school, mostly from the city, pleasure that, what Hartford society and St. Peter's had resumed, out of novelty, or on principle, had never become obsolete among the villagers of Hebron and neighboring towns. The local Saturday night, at the town hall, alternated *round dances* and *square,* the latter accompanied by the dry squeak of the village fiddler, while the figures were called out by an ancient practitioner.

Sometimes charades were the order of the evening. Once Professor Daniel Mornet of the Sorbonne was paying a brief visit upon Dr. Krappe, our learned folklorist. A gracious, lithe, aging little figure, Mornet easily yielded to my decanal plea, and, in his native French (which none of his auditors could do more than read), improvised eloquent greetings and salutations from the Sorbonne to its sister institution, the School of Liberal and Human Studies. Even more charmingly flexible of him was Mornet's vivacious participation in the evening's charades; it was like Turgenev's on Sunday evenings at Mme. Viardot's. The young Henry James, as I remembered, saw in Turgenev's conduct "that spontaneity which Europeans have and we have not. Fancy Longfellow, Lowell, or Charles Norton doing the like, and every Sunday evening!"

Often the evening pleasure provided was a picnic. The Pendleton sisters knew all the abandoned roads—proper roads for walking, the like of which my part of Massachusetts had lost; and they knew the local ponds (not yet glorified into "lakes")and the local boulders and deserted houses. They were also experts at baked beans in the Connecticut style—made of yellow-eyes, rich with molasses and salt pork, and kept in the oven of the old wood-fire stove till the beans had richly coagulated.

Benny and I took anti-Protestant pleasure in having two services on each weekday but only one—a sung mass (Merbecke or the *Missa de Angelis*) on Sunday. In the fashion of Europe, as we delighted to think, after morning mass the rest of the day was free for any innocent pleasure —for a swimming party or a picnic supper. It was on Sunday that, one year, the married Pendleton sister, Mrs. Gilbert, the "Martha"among them, engineered a picnic with the pious intent of having all the members work, with scythes and shears, clearing the brush from the pre-Revolutionary Anglican cemetery where the first rector was buried. The labor was strenuous—at least for city folk and artists; but at dusk a fire was built and "wienies"roasted in one corner of the graveyard.

By ten, or ten-thirty, the Pendleton sisters and other older members of the school had disappeared, and the public entertainment came to an end. But the night was not over; and the young people, in twos or threes, generally set off into the unlit country roads, walking at rapid pace and talking with at least equal rapidity.

It mattered little to some of the younger students, but to the founders, the school's intellectual position was the primary and chief concern. Just as we annexed new eligibles to the membership each year, so we developed our doctrine. Though Chesterton's *Orthodoxy* did not often appear in the reading list, it perhaps best represents—along with the *American Review*, not published until the 1930s—the general position toward which we found our way. What we stood for, we would then, perhaps, have called classicism or humanism; but neomedievalism and regionalism are (retrospectively, at least) perhaps more proper names.

"St. Peter's people" were anti-industrialist and, like the English distributists, Chesterton and Belloc, were neither finance capitalists nor socialists. Intellectually, they were antispecialists. Three British "prophets" who, writing in the nineteenth century, denounced the directions taken by their time were Ruskin, Arnold, and Newman; and the spirits of these high rebels against "progress" certainly hovered persistently over the school.

The school never grew much in size: the numbers, including lecturers and nonlecturers, never exceeded thirty. But it grew in strength and solidity; and its best years were from 1926 through 1930. It was in 1926 that my friend, Mr. Hite, the professor of philosophy at New-Church Theological School, began his lectures on Greek philosophy. Then, as I was returning from a European summer vacation in 1926, I made on shipboard the acquaintance of Professor and Mrs. Eugene Chase, both New Englanders, both Democrats and Episcopalians, and about Benny's age and mine. Eugene, a former Rhodes Scholar and a Ph.D. from Harvard, had been professor of political science at Wesleyan, and now was professor at Lafayette College. The Chases, I immediately, and correctly, saw to be proper St. Peter's people. In the summer of 1929 Eugene became one of our regular lecturers; and within a year or two the couple bought and restored and made their summer home a fine old house on the outskirts of Hebron. Mrs. Chase, Ann, a Radcliffe graduate, was a poet and an intellectual of fine sensitive speech—at once delicately beautiful and keen witted. Also, at about this time, my distant cousin, Edward Flint, a Harvard graduate who had majored in philosophy and mathematics and who was also an organist and organ builder, joined our regular summer community and made himself intellectually, musically, socially indispensable. The last summer session of the school, the ninth, held in 1931, when the founders, Benny and I, were both in England, was operated by Eugene Chase as president and Edward Flint as dean.

Beside the resident lecturers, others came for shorter periods. Morse Allen, a Princeton Ph.D. who was professor of English at Trinity College, Hartford, drove down almost every year to give two or three lectures: he, who took much interest in contemporary poetry, was a friend of Miss Susan's and Helen's. At the ninth session, Howard Hinnerds, professor of music at Wellesley, and Cornelius Kruse, professor of philosophy at Wesleyan, lectured. And from time to time, we had visits, concerts, and classes—one of them in the folksong, European as well as British—from Wellington Sloane, a graduate of the Yale Department of Music, whose friendship Benny had formed during his own Yale period. Sloane was a gifted and brilliant pianist, also a personality of ebullience, independence, and gaiety—at once arrogant (a "genius") and disarming.

For students, as distinct from regular or occasional lecturers, we had some groups of young college people, chiefly women. Three of my Boston University students—one Irish, one Jewish, one Yankee (and Unitarian) came for several years; so did some young women, Jewish, Irish, and Yankee, whose friendship Helen Gilbert had formed during a recent year of study at Columbia. And Helen had a Congregational cousin, a young woman who was a student at the other recently founded Connecticut College at New London. Of young men, I remember especially two, both in their twenties—one, a young philosopher; the other a young Greek scholar: both, and particularly the Hellenist, also violinists. So there was a generational group of the young who combined culture with a country holiday—such a group as existed also at Brook Farm, the transcendentalist analogy to our school.

How and why did the school come to end—as an existence, a visible small group of people meeting for two weeks each summer in a small Connecticut village? Well, its sequence had been interrupted by the year Benny and I had both been in England. From that year, I returned to Boston; but Benny, who continued his priestly ministrations in England, became a British citizen and the vicar of a parish in Bedfordshire, did not. The school had been our joint enterprise, the offspring of our close friendship. It represented to us a meeting of minds, a doctrinal position slowly worked out through winters of letter writing; it was not, for us, what it seemed to Hebronians, even to the Pendleton sisters, a summer idyll—half serious, half a kind of game or play.

Finally, however, the decision to give up the school was mine, as the work of making the enterprise run had always been. Benny, our theoretician, was deficient in energy, physical and nervous. Never, even in my youth, did I have much stamina; but, by unrelaxed intensity, I could lecture, play the organ twice daily, attempt to reconcile the sometimes clashing temperaments of the community's geniuses—all that for the space of a fortnight. That concentrated exertion exhausted me, however, for the rest of the summer, which, during those years of the twenties, I spent on my father's farm: my father, who could scarcely not notice my exhaustion, used to say because of that, "I hate St. Peter's School." If I so used up my summer—the teacher's special blessing, I had no strength with which to write. By the time I returned from England, I was already the author of one book, was in the midst of another, and had done the research which was intended to end in a third. Almost everything in life is a matter of priorities: I could not, on however modest a scale, be both an administrator and at the same time write my books. So the school, unavoidably, and without much struggle over the decision, had to go.

The school, after all, had meant most to me. "The song comes back most to the singer." The school, a creative enterprise, both in thinking out doctrine and in personal relationships, learning how to live with other intense people, was the matrix of all I subsequently was and did. All I later became, as a person, teacher, and writer, grew out of my participation in the school. It was my first central effort at finding my vocation.

6

Early Teaching: At Three Universities

I went off, at twenty-one, to the University of Kentucky, never having taught before and terrified by the books I had read on the problems of teaching. Lexington was a city of about fifty thousand in those days, a far larger city than I had ever lived in. As I was ready to set out, my mother gave me postage stamps to use on letters home. That may have been done simply to be sure that I would have no excuse not to write, but I guessed it was prompted by her feeling that Kentucky, being so far from New England, was frontier territory, and might lack a post office.

I was offered fifteen hundred dollars to teach at Lexington, and, presumably because I had run short of money at the end of the summer, I wrote or wired the dean that traveling expenses be paid. The dean's reply was to the effect that such a misapprehension on my part of how universities were run raised doubts about my judgment, whether I was mature enough for my post. But the dean's doubts proved groundless; I satisfactorily discharged my duties, and was invited to return.

I taught fifteen hours a week, of which three were given to a group of engineering students and three to sophomores in a survey course using as its text *The Century Readings in English Literature*, the first, I think, of such college anthologies. The remaining hours were filled in with Freshman Composition, three sections of it. With the students I had no difficulties, not even with the engineers, the most sophisticated of them. I read and graded the "themes"conscientiously. The literary course was given me as dessert, and so I found it. Though I had studied the same anthology

during my sophomore year at Wesleyan, I saw for myself that no
one really reads unless he reads to teach or to write criticism.

The typical problems I had read about in the textbooks on
education never arose, or never arose when they could be seen as
situations. I had to use my wits, also my common sense and judgment (neither of them my strongest trait, though I did not totally
lack them), also my intuition, imagination, empathy, and enthusiasm for the humanities, in all of which I relatively abounded.

If I had never taught before, in a formal sense, I had all my life
been eager to learn and was now eager enough to impart my doctrines and enthusiasms to any who would listen. If I had never
taught before, I had learned to speak in public, at Christian Endeavor groups and weekday prayer meetings; I had served on
church "Gospel Teams," and I had, in high school, debated. And,
for sheer human relations, I had directed the volunteer adult choir
of the East Hampton church. All these instances suggest that,
given the support of a post, an office, a platform, I could overcome
my shyness and self-consciousness. I had a "relationship"; and
within that prescribed and accepted relationship, I could function.

I had vaguely drifted both into teaching, and into teaching
English. When I left Wesleyan, I had no more definite conception
of what I wanted to be than to be a gentleman and a scholar and
an artist and a saint; an order as vague as large. What would I have
done or become, had I had independent means? Perhaps a dilettante; but I think my New England conscience would have kept
me from anything quite so irresponsible. I would have felt the
moral and social responsibility to do something for society—morally to earn my right to live, even if I hadn't had to earn my
livelihood. Probably in the course of time I would have found my
vocation in writing, with all the implications that word has come
to have for me—self-definition, salvation through self-definition,
sharing those discoveries with those who have hearing ears. But it
is good that I had first to find, and honorably to practice, a profession. Actually confronted with young men and women, reasonably
docile and amiable, and presented with the duties of teaching them
to write literate prose and to read the "sacred texts" of English
literature, I responded; I accepted a responsibility by the faithful
discharge of which I could honorably support myself.

In Lexington, my Yankee self was transplanted into the southern world. Even though not that of the Deep South, it was a world
much more relaxed and easygoing than the world in which I had
been reared. Then, and ever thereafter, I felt at home with men

reared in Kentucky, Tennessee, and Virginia, and they with me; at least this has been so with the literary and intellectual men of those states. Were they as sincere as Yankees? Perhaps not as rigorously so; for they were, all of them, far more social; attached more importance to gracious manners, the rituals of which soften the contacts and conflicts between naked egos. Unlike my regional compatriots, their first impulse, when an invitation to a party, or an experience, was offered, was not to say "No."Manners, politics, and religion were their world. Of the importance of manners and breeding, I was not then yet aware, and I was totally uninterested in practical politics, which, like the WASPS among whom I had been reared, I then regarded as dirty business. But I could communicate with them on religion and literature; and I envied them their manners.

That year in Lexington I shared a room in a private house with a young instructor in economics, a Middle Westerner, already engaged to be married—a sober, sensible young man who was rarely in the room. The family with whom we lived were Baptists; and a scrap of anecdote remains with me. It depends for its point on that popular southern religion, which shared its popularity in Lexington with the sect grandly and superdenominationally called by its adherents the Christian Church and by others the Campbellite. Mischievously, I one day quoted to the little daughter of the house the words of Agrippa to St. Paul: "Almost thou persuades me to be a Christian," to which she vigorously, even violently, replied, "I'll never be anything but a Baptist."

My roommate and I took our meals at a boardinghouse nearby; and here I was first treated to what I took to be southern food, of which I remember the beaten biscuits, not quite the treat they were alleged to be, and the vegetables all floating in some kind of fat or grease. Except for chicken or ham, I probably didn't eat the meat; for in those days I supposed myself to be a vegetarian— which really simply meant that I abhorred thick bloody slices of rare beef. The food was probably simple country fare; it was at any event better than the cheap and ill-cooked rations my fraternity brothers and I ate at Wesleyan.

From the boardinghouse, I often had welcome relief. A cultivated Jewish lady, Bianca Noa, reared in Germany, and a graduate of the Leipzig Conservatory, took an almost immediate liking to me; and I had an admirably cooked dinner two or three times a week at her house, preceded or followed by a piano lesson.

She disclaimed having any such natural musicality or musical talent as she attributed to me, but she felt, accurately, that I had no proper technical grounding. Up till that time I had played merely the easier kind of Romantic music, in which the right hand does all the work, and the pedal serves to cover imprecisions. She immediately set me to study Bach's *Two and Three-Part Inventions,* in which the left hand has to be as firm, clear, and decisive as the right hand.

These were not my only musical activities. The wife of the head of the English department, Mrs. Dantzler, was a contralto of admirable voice and schooling; and during my year at Lexington, I served as her steady accompanist. Her repertory was that of the German lieder. She did not sing Hugo Wolf, but she did sing admirably and with understanding the other classics of that kind— Franz Schubert, Schumann, and Brahms. Though I had first known the lieder at Wesleyan, where I had accompanied two professorial wives, this new work did much to fortify my faith.

I was also, at fifty dollars a month, choir director of a large church, the Central Christian. I would have preferred to play the organ as well as direct, but a gray-haired woman was already installed at the console, playing —though not very well; and, though quite aware of my desire, she explicitly declined to make way for me.

The University of Kentucky had a modest symphony orchestra directed by Professor Karl Lambert, a sound old German. The orchestra was not complete enough in its repertory of instruments to dispense with the piano as a filler-in, and I was invited to provide that. I took special pleasure in playing the piano support to Mozart's Symphony in G Minor.

The whole life at Lexington was easy and friendly. There were no distinctions observed between instructors and full professors; and, on more than one occasion, I was a guest at the house of the president, Dr. McVey, a cultivated southern gentleman.

Toward the end of my year at Harvard, the cost of which had been saved out of my Kentucky year of teaching and choir directing and inexpensive living, I had again to find a post. Chairmen, or their delegates, from universities in search of instructors, came to Harvard in the spring to interview candidates. It was my good fortune to be interviewed by Joseph Warren Beach, of the University of Minnesota, who engaged me to teach three sections of freshmen at a salary of eighteen hundred dollars.

Minneapolis was a delightful city to live in—large enough to have a real symphony orchestra, an excellent School of Music functioning as part of the university, department stores and book-stores; and the university itself was a real university, with so large and able a faculty and such a range of types among its students that I felt immediately enriched. As a provincial New Englander, I had no idea of the high quality of the great western state universi-ties, to which we had, indeed, no New England equivalent. The University of Minnesota was more the equivalent of Harvard than of Wesleyan; and, I came to the conclusion, it would have given me not only a better formal academic education but a range of intellectual and spiritual fathers and congenial contemporaries such as I did not find at Wesleyan.

I rented a large front bedroom on the East River Road, over-looking the Mississippi. My landlady was a prematurely widowed woman of Irish extraction, a devout Roman Catholic, whom I found congenial, as I did the only other lodger, Gregory Breit, a young Austrian physicist. Across the street lived Professor Karl Iashley, later at Harvard, an eventually famous biologist with a musical wife, with whom I used, weekly, to play four-hand tran-scriptions for the piano of Beethoven's symphonies. I took my meals at the excellent small restaurants in the Latin Quarter, the neighborhood of the university.

As for my teaching, I was allowed remarkably free rein. The textbooks, in composition and in literature, were assigned, and the same for all sections of Freshman English; but each instructor fol-lowed his own methods. Strongly influenced by my year of study with Babbitt at Harvard, I adapted his method and sought to spread his brand of what I regarded as Christian humanism or classicism. Each day I wrote on the blackboard one or more maxims drawn sometimes from the poets but more often from the sages and the saints. The sentence might be from Confucius, the *Bhagavad Gita*, Marcus Aurelius, *The Imitation of Christ*, Plato or Aristotle. One day I wrote from Plato, "The unexamined life is not the truly human life." Before I began the lesson for the day—prescribed by an outline as a part of the standard freshman course—I used to give a little homily developing the religious or humanistic maxims on the blackboard.

This habit once brought me into serious trouble. As early as 1922 I happened upon Aldous Huxley in the university library, read *Crome Yellow*, and interpreted it, properly enough, in the light of Huxley's subsequent development, as an exposure of the futility and despair of naturalism. One morning I read aloud to my class of freshmen the fifth chapter of *Crome Yellow*—the barnyard chapter which began by describing a sow suckling her brood. One, at least, of my female students reported this to her mother; I was summoned gravely into the office of the acting chairman of the department. I answered, in perfect innocence and confidence, that I had read the passage as a part of my regular readings in religion and humanism. The acting chairman, the distinguished Shakespearean scholar and critic E. E. Stoll, was convinced of my innocence but also of my naïveté; and he told me that, in view of the lack of judgment which this showed, my contract would not be renewed for more than a year. He assured me that, as a man of the world, he understood all these things and did not himself think the passage I had read obscene, but that "We have to consider the students and parents." At the moment I took all this quite blandly, assuring Professor Stoll that I had no intention of staying at Minnesota more than an additional year anyway, since after that I planned to take my doctorate. The additional year was granted me, and passed off without further need of rebuke from authority.

I must have been an instructor at Minnesota when the English department was at its height. It included not only Professors Klaeber, Stoll, and Beach, but, as assistant professors, people like Marjorie Nicholson, and W. D. Dunn, author of an excellent book on Sir Thomas Browne, early a favorite author of mine.

My first year at Minnesota was memorable by a friendship with Professor Joseph Warren Beach, a brilliant scholar and critic who was even more extraordinary as a human being. He was clear in his judgments, delicate in the application of them. An acknowledged atheist, he was empathic enough to be able to teach Newman as though from within. Though he never disguised from me his denial of revealed religion, he was so aware of my religious convictions and my need of religion that he never attempted to argue me out of my faith.

But Beach was indeed admirable in his dealings with all the young. He must then have been around forty, was in poor health, was writing his distinguished critical books, *The Method of Henry James*, for one, yet he always had time for graduate students and bright undergraduates. Every Sunday afternoon there was an informal tea party at his house open to any bright young people who wanted to come; and these were occasions to be remembered for the deference he paid his juniors, the delicacy and skill with which he drew out the characteristic tone and timbre of each. He was the orchestra leader, not the soloist.

When I was bleeding from the rebuke administered to me by Mr. Stoll, I naturally went to Mr. Beach to have him bind up the wounds, and that he did most gently and affectionately. To parallel the pains of my "awkward age," he told me of the suffering he went through during his own years at Harvard Graduate School—how, night after night, he would run the racetracks with tears streaming down his face.

At the end of my first year, when Beach was putting his house to rights before going off for a sabbatical in Italy, he assembled for me a gift of twenty-five books from his library, the books selected comprising a perspective portrait of me as I then was, and of my interests. The books included a volume or two of Pater, two little volumes of William Dean Howells's farces, a critical book on Howells which Beach had reviewed and which was covered with his painstaking marginalia and, even, indexed, and, finally, a morocco-bound copy of Dante in Italian. Mr. Beach was the first highly civilized man I had known.

By my second year at Minnesota, I had adequately enough mastered the texts taught in Freshman English to be able to afford a variety of intra- and extracurricular activities. I took an evening extension course in Italian with Professor Ruth Shepard Phelps, a beautiful and elegant lady with whom, legend had it, the deceased poet Arthur Upson had been in love; and I took two graduate courses—a seminar in Plato with Professor David F. Swenson, a lifelong disciple of Kierkegaard, and one in the History of Drama with Professor Firkins.

Oscar Firkins had once been a member of the English department; but, having no taste for committees and organized activities, he had, by the time I knew him, been constituted a one-man Department of Comparative Literature.

Firkins seemed to me a genius. Unmarried, nearly blind, he lived with his aged mother and his spinster sisters, one of whom was a librarian. He knew many languages, but could use his eyes only a few hours a day; he had therefore trained his mother and his sisters to read aloud to him in languages which they could but pronounce—a case with some analogies to Milton's. Mr. Firkins had for a year been dramatic critic for the New York *Nation*. He was himself a minor playwright as well as the author of three or four excellent if highly mannered books: one on Emerson, one on Jane Austen, and one on Howells. His course in drama gave a quarter to the period from classical antiquity to Ibsen, a quarter to Ibsen, and a quarter to drama since Ibsen (including Chekhov and O'Neill).

His method of teaching was unique. He began each hour by dictating a digest of the preceding day's lecture, which students were to take down into their notebooks. This digest was, in effect, a highly literary essay—the title carefully chosen, the style precious, the punctuation (also dictated) very close. After the dictation was over, Mr. Firkins lectured freely, often with his eyes half closed: indeed, he never seemed aware of his crowded classroom. My fountain pen raced as rapidly as it could, trying to take down the extemporized lecture, which was scarcely, if at all, inferior to what had been so meticulously dictated.

At Minnesota, I found men in the higher ranks to whom I could pay real respect and homage, men who were full professors not in title only (titles which, after the fashion of Harvard they did not use, any more than they used their degree of doctor), professors who were also men of substance and personal distinction.

Both years, but especially the second, I made many friends among my students and my fellow instructors and with graduate students. I had all around me attractive and talented young men and women of my own age—some of them literary, some painters, some musicians—Celius Daugherty, a pianist who rose to subsequent distinction, among them.

I was particularly drawn to Johan Egilsrud, a young Swede whose father was a physician and whose impressive mother, high in the ranks of Theosophists, had her own private chapel with its gilded harmonium. Johan was the most civilized man of my own age I had met, as Beach was the most civilized elder. Johan's dress, elegantly tailored, his spats and his walking stick, impressed me. So did his well-bred, easy manners, his general possession of style. He was the perfect dilettante, aesthete, man of the world. He was facilely voluble in three or four languages; he spoke none of them well, but all of them without embarrassment. He also played the piano and painted and wrote poetry—none of them very well either; they were accomplishments, not of course meant to be professional. Full of charm, he possessed his own kind of integrity, too. I was, by comparison, crude, an enthusiast, earnest and intense—as well as more masculine and ambitious. I could admire him as a work of art, and wish to incorporate his urbanities, without suffering the self-destruction of envy.

There followed the two years at Princeton, where I clumsily

attempted to imitate the dress and style of Johan and to hold fast to the orthodox humanism of Babbitt while acquiring the scholarly technique which my major professor, Dr. Root, was so urbanely skillful in imparting. As I was about to take my doctorate, I had again to think—and now more seriously—of a college post. Partly because of the smaller size of the Princeton Graduate School, fewer openings were referred to it than, say, to Harvard. I learned of but three. Dr. Root, impressed by my Pope dissertation, offered me a temporary year's instructorship at Princeton, with the possibility of its being made a more lasting appointment, if I did well. But I turned his kind offer down, both because of its temporary character and because, by then, I had enough of Princeton—partially described by T. K. Whipple, one of its literary doctors, as "a mixture of Oxford and Cranford," and by Stuart Sherman as "that brave little city striving to be Oxford among the New Jersey oil refineries." It was certainly a place where wealth and social position were necessary if one were to live the real Princeton life.

There was a vacancy at Williams College for which Mr. Root nominated me, and I journeyed there for a weekend to find myself at a miniature Princeton with the further disadvantage of its being located in a village. I must have seemed either gauche or not duly deferential to constituted authority, for I had not the chance of refusing the post—a refusal I trust I would have had the judgment to make.

There was a third possibility. Dr. Root had a request from Boston University, to which had recently gone, as chairman, a medievalist of whom he thought well. And my heart leapt at the thought of living in Boston, which I have always called my native city. I accepted the offer.

I went to Boston University at twenty-six hundred dollars a year, a salary on which I could have afforded to rent an apartment. But I was so used to frugal living that, instead, I rented a room a few blocks from the college, in a dismal, rundown neighborhood so near the railroad track that my room was soot infested when I opened the window. Luncheon I could eat with my fellow instructors; but, married, they departed to their suburban homes and wives at the end of the teaching day. My dinners were solitary; and so, chiefly, were the plays and movies I took in after dinner.

For the next three years I shared an apartment in Cambridge with my grandmother Dillingham, now widowed after two happy marriages. This was not a fortunate arrangement, close as we had been to each other in earlier years. She had sold her stately house in Auburndale, was transplanted from her house and her congenial circle of friends to the anonymity of a new apartment house in a characterless suburban area—I cannot call it a neighborhood. Now she was alone all day; and when I came home from Boston, tired after my arduous day of teaching, she was eager to have me to keep her company, to be her talkative and appreciative companion, a kind of substitute for her husbands. She was growing old, and I was no longer in such awe of her. My own wings of ambition were sprouting; my own interests, theological, musical, and literary actively developing. She sought to close the generation gap; but it could not be closed. I felt confined and cribbed—a feeling not helped by our regularly going across the street for dinner at a genteel boardinghouse where I was the youngest guest and where most of the company were elderly women.

When I was at home, I had student papers to read, classes to prepare, and I was beginning to write essays and reviews for publication. One morning, in my room, I was reading Dostoyevsky's *Brothers Karamazov*, in preparation for teaching it to a class. My grandmother looked at the book; and perhaps noticed that it was mostly in dialogue; asked me what it was. When she identified my reading as a novel, she, remembering the rules under which she was reared, that novels were for amusement and to be read only after the day's work was done, protested: "Why, Austin, you are not reading a novel in the morning?" Upon that, I reared myself to my professional literary-critical height and replied, "A great novel like Dostoyevsky's has to be read in the morning; for it calls upon my fullest range, my imagination and feelings as well as my mind. At night, when tired, I can read criticism or theology, for those I can read with the top of my head, but not a great novel or a great poem." To this kind of pronouncement or credo, heatedly asserted, she was at a loss for a reply.

To my grandmother, in the diminution of her life, I was never, I think, cruel, but I dared not be too indulgent. Fortunately, this period of our cohabitation was not infinitely extended. Toward the end of our third year, while visiting my father at Littleton, she had a heart attack and died instantly. I played the organ at her church funeral, as I had done at the funeral of my grandfather Dillingham.

During those years, Boston University occupied a miscellaneous group of buildings, most of them near Copley Square. In 1926, and for long thereafter, it had four English departments, each with its own head and staff. And mine was the ignominy of teaching not at the Liberal Arts College but at the College of Practical

Arts and Letters, "discovered and founded" by T. Lawrence Davis, himself a graduate from the Boston University College of Business Administration. Boston University itself was coeducational; but Dean Davis, a schemer and promoter, conceived the idea of a college within the university to be limited exclusively to women, a kind of female counterpart of the College of Business Administration and a kind of rival to the already existing and in its way excellent Simmons College.

The college at which I taught was, in effect, a glorified secretarial school. It offered a four-year course leading to the degree of Bachelor of Secretarial Science. The chief staff, one might say, consisted of teachers of typing and shorthand; later, courses on commercial art were added. There were a few courses in French and Spanish. There was a psychologist, an economist, and a part-time philosopher, lent from the College of Liberal Arts. General culture was the province of the English department.

I had only contempt for the dean of the college, a petty tyrant with no understanding of the principles of education and no interest in them. The real work of the office and in a sense of the college was handled by his devoted secretary.

The president of the university was almost equally distasteful to me. He inaugurated convocation services, which were held for the whole university at Phillips Brooks's and H. H. Richardson's Trinity Church in Copley Square. On these occasions he delivered commemorative addresses on the founders and the cofounders of Boston University, orations which equaled, in panegyric, Bossuet's on the death of Queen Henrietta Maria of England. One memorable address was devoted to Mr. and Mrs. Stetson, cofounders, whose single and conjoined virtues were likened, through many paragraphs, to a pair of majestic rivers flowing first in rich singleness and then in fertile confluence. It was in the same memorable address Dr. Marsh delighted me by recalling the testimony of Mrs. Stetson, offered to him when he called on her at the Hotel Vendome, that there were two books which she read daily: her Bible and her stock market report. Truly, this was, to use one of Dr. Marsh's favorite phrases from St. Paul, an "elect lady."

The faculty were all dragooned into attending these convocation services, as they were also forced by some kind of intimidation to attend the commencement exercises in the incongruous setting of the Boston Arena. On these occasions I listened with particular loathing to the citations of honorary degrees, citations which must have been written by the president himself—citations which, almost exclusively, celebrated the virtues of the prominent leaders of business and finance who might be expected to contribute money to a greater Boston University.

Dean Davis, for his part, had his own weekly convocations at the college, at which a motley group of people orated or performed: perhaps a Baptist clergyman from Brookline who drooled over "Bobbie" Burns at the convocation nearest the anniversary of Burns's birth; perhaps a lady who specialized in teaching ballet to children, a withered hag who marshaled her troops of urchins on the platform of the college. There was a pipe organ in the college auditorium on which I had some pleasure in practicing Bach and Mendelssohn; but my talent was officially turned to account on various occasions by having me play for community singing such classics as "Pack Up Your Troubles in Your Old Kit Bag."

Here was a world, allegedly academic, which was obviously repellent, even painful to me. It took inner resources to endure it. Boston University was, beyond comparison, inferior to the University of Kentucky, let alone the great University of Minnesota. And it was grossly as well as precisely the opposite of Princeton. If Princeton seemed too unnaturally refined (I might almost say "too un-American"), BUPAL was too crude. Yet it was down-to-earth, the hard blunt world; and, after Princeton, I felt the need of something gritty and "challenging" (a word I never liked, though I responded to, even craved, the thing). But to survive in that world of the practical arts, I had to develop not only a sense of humor but a strong taste for the grotesque—the one aesthetic mode capable of disinfecting vulgarity by stylizing it.

From the beginning of my stay at Boston University, I was given, as a relief from my heavy schedule of teaching freshmen and sophomores, a course in Creative Writing, which met around a seminar table; and this course I continued to teach as long as I was at Boston University. Though none of my pupils ever became name writers, such a class certainly drew the most gifted and engaging girls in the college—Jewish, Irish, Greek, with an occasional Yankee, one of them a cultivated Yankee Unitarian. These were girls who should have gone to a liberal arts college, but who somehow lacked the right requirements, had failed to take enough Latin or mathematics in high school.

When I began my first class in Creative Writing, I was still a more or less rigid disciple of Irving Babbitt. The classical counsel I derived from my sage and which I tried to impart to my pupils was: write universally; but after a few weeks I realized how futile it was to tell writers to write universally. No one can write like Shakespeare or Sophocles or Dante by intent and will. All one can enjoin upon young writers is to express themselves honestly, and to write out of themselves; it is not up to them whether the self they express overlaps other selves deeply and widely enough for critics to call them universal. *Universal* is a time-honored critical term, and it is of some use to critics; but concern with it can only harm creative writers, whom it can only prompt to the production of stereotypes.

For several years at Boston University I also directed the glee club, which I did not allow to sing the kind of music which glee clubs had sung in my Wesleyan days. Mine did Russian songs, folksongs, and Elizabethan madrigals like Orlando Gibbons's "The Silver Swan."

My early years of teaching at Boston University were mostly unhappy. But there was the relief that the college was a college of commuters; that, when the day's work was over, I was free to depart into my own intellectual and spiritual world. During my weekends, I was not troubled by the importunities of past, present, and future students. Once I had left the College of Practical Arts, I was at liberty to be as impractical as I wished: I played the piano, read copiously, went to church, and wrote—theological essays and reviews.

It is a handicap to a professor to have to be a professor whether inside the classroom or out, whether on the campus (in this case nonexistent), or in the street. And this handicap I was spared. Outside the college building and the stated hours of instruction and conferences, I was an anonymous citizen. About Boston I felt as Robert Herrick did about London or as St. Paul did of Tarsus: that I was a citizen of no mean city. I could not have survived these years had they been in a campus college of the same mediocre standards. The blessing was that outside of the classroom I could feel myself to be a scholar, an artist, even, in my modest way, a man of the world.

7

Europe: A Year of Independence

ॐ

In 1927, at the age of twenty-eight, I had never been farther into civilization than Boston. Out of my first year's pay from Boston University, I had saved a thousand dollars with which to take advantage of the glories and grandeurs of Europe. I had a step-aunt, if I can call her that, the daughter of my grandmother Warren's second husband, who taught at the exclusive Miss Porter's School in Framingham, Connecticut. In her young days, Frances Dillingham had thought of herself as a writer. She had published two books of stories for children, which I read with pleasure, and some stories of New England village life, somewhat in the style of Mary E. Wilkins.

Aunt Frances was a fellow teacher with Irving Babbitt's sister Kate at Miss Porter's School; but her special friend was a vivacious Miss Mellor, her contemporary but not her equal in mind, I felt. For some affluent years Aunt Frances and Miss Mellor had annually spent their summers in Europe; and on this summer they invited me to join them. Their own tastes, though refined, were eclectic.

Aunt Frances and I sat down over our maps, and I was generously allowed to share in the planning of this summer's itinerary myself. What we mapped out was, in effect, a kind of eighteenth-century grand tour, including London, Canterbury, Oxford, Ely, and Cambridge, Eton and Windsor Palace, Paris, Chartres, the châteaux of the Loire, Italy, Milan, Rome, and Florence—a journey up the Rhine from Heidelberg to Cologne, the Belgian Venice, Bruges, and Switzerland, Lausanne, the Lion of Lucerne and the Castle of Chillon included. All this was got into two months.

Though Aunt Frances was, to appearance, an impractical lady, it was she who managed the party's business affairs, including the choice of the hotels and pensions we should stay at; and every evening after dinner, we had a business meeting at which the day's expenses were divided into three, and the troublesome translation then made of American dollars into foreign currency.

Miss Mellor had little taste for churches and art galleries; Aunt Frances "did" them all with a superficial thoroughness to which I felt patronizingly superior. She looked in turn at every celebrated masterpiece, registered its subject and the name of the painter, then walked out into the piazza. But I was allowed to linger over both churches and paintings while the aunts took their English afternoon tea.

For me, of course, the churches were the great attractions. Our party reached Paris early one afternoon; and before dinner I had already visited Notre Dame. Everywhere we went, I rushed into churches—somewhat shocked, to be sure, to find in Italy groups of tourists being guided around the church, or walking around on their own and chatting while mass was going on at one or more altars, and to discover the absence of worshipers in the English cathedrals, most of which had a sign affixed to one chapel, "This chapel reserved for prayer and meditation," as though the whole of the church weren't intended for just that purpose.

Switzerland was the favorite of my aunts; it was not mine. I found it all too neat, clean, and pretty; I preferred the picturesque disorder of Italy. I was distressed to see the old cathedral in Lausanne turned into a Calvinist church, with whitewashed interior. Not only was the chancel empty, but, to make matters worse, the pews had been diverted from facing the chancel to facing toward the long left wall, from which was suspended the pulpit, the center of worship. As for the mountains and lakes of Switzerland, my comment was that they looked exactly like Woolworth colored postcards. A young disciple of mine, traveling by train through the Alps a few years later, pulled down all the window shades so as to shut out the garish glories.

On this first journey to the land of Europe, the land of culture, all in the past, I wanted everything to be Gothic, though I did have discernment enough to admire the Norman cathedral of Ely. In painting, I admired the Botticellis at Florence, to which Pater had introduced me, the Fra Angelicos, also at Florence, and the Memlings at Bruges; I had then no least taste for the baroque.

This grand tour of Europe was meant but as a preliminary

survey. It was evident that I would return as soon as I could—to
Italy, France, and England—every summer if possible. But soon the
chance came for a year abroad. I was already planning a book on
the seventeenth-century English poet, Crashaw, and for that I required a year in England. I applied for a Guggenheim, and, at the
suggestion of my Princeton sponsor, Professor Root, for one of the
fellowships which the American Council of Learned Societies had
just founded. With Root's backing, I was awarded one of the latter.
The fellowship paid eighteen hundred dollars, with an additional
three or five hundred for travel expenses. In the management of
these funds I was so scrupulous that, having lived for a year and
traveled on the eighteen hundred dollars, I returned unspent the
extra stipend, receiving in return a puzzled rebuke from the sensible young man who was the foundation's secretary.

My journals of the year in London abound in the self-examina-
tion and self-excoriations so customary in my journals generally;
yet this was much the happiest year I had yet experienced—my
annus mirabilis I used to call it.

The only real trouble I suffered in England was dietary. The
English are heavy eaters, and eaters, chiefly, of rare beef—nearly
raw meat; and I, who was a vegetarian in theory and nearly so in
practice, found the meals the hardest thing to manage. Breakfast,
since it consisted of oatmeal, eggs, toast, and coffee, and the four
o'clock tea with its slices of buttered bread thinner than any
American can cut them, gave me pleasure. But how could I manage lunch and especially dinner? Simpson's on the Strand was not
for me. Chiefly, I took dinner at the Lyons Corner House, or at
some pub, where I could have a sharp Welsh Rabbit and a glass of
stout, the black English brew. So I managed. But it remained puzzling to me how English clergy and scholars and other intellectuals
and gentlemen could be so gross, so materialistic, in their eating,
and yet so high and fine in their thinking.

But English eccentricity and English variety of types brought
me only relief and delight. Shelley was an Englishman as well as
Cobbett; Dame Edith Sitwell, as English as Churchill. Eccentrics
in England are not really eccentrics. In America, the clergy and the
professors are expected to look and behave like businessmen; and
their only resource in opposition is to be bizarre and bohemian.
But in England men of contemplative professions, men who have
gone to the university, need not appear like traders and plough-
men. They ride bicycles, wear beards, speak in the mandarin dia-
lect of Oxford. No one thinks the less of them for their eccentricity

if they are good in their own line and are accredited by their peers. The result of this allowance is to remove an immense burden from the shoulders of the intellectual, leaving him free to pursue his own vocation.

For me, to be in England was immediately to be relieved of the American burden of conformity. I wasn't grotesquely eccentric, but I was free to be—if I had my mind to my own main concern.

The English, however, are not all eccentrics or intellectuals. While America is divided between its highbrows and lowbrows, England has a large group of middlebrows, of common readers. With us, almost all the intellectuals are themselves writers, and readers of others' books; but in England there was still, I found, a large group of people who, without any ambition to write or even particularly to keep up with current literature, as a professional literary obligation, yet read widely and subscribed to the *Times Literary Supplement* or to the *Times* Book of the Month Club. At the White Hall, the modest residential hotel in Bloomsbury where I lived most of my London year, I knew many such.

I was fortified in not being in England alone. My old friend, Benny Bissell, had just been ordained priest in the Episcopal Church, but had been unable to find an American appointment. He decided to go to England with me, taking his chance on picking up employment there; and there he succeeded. During the first few months I was in London, he served as curate to a cultivated old vicar who might have appeared in Trollope—a vicar in Farnham, a country parish only about an hour from London. I used to spend weekends with him. In a few months he had built up a delectable circle which included that traditional British character, the retired East India colonel, and a cultivated old lady.

Then, after the first three months, he came to London as curate to a celebrated Anglo-Catholic parish, St. John's, Waterloo, just across the bridge. Father Hutchinson, the vicar of St. John's, who looked rather Spanish than English, was a celibate who came of a family of actors and was himself of dramatic gifts. His friends and acquaintances included everyone from the Prince of Wales to young men recently released from jail, whom he temporarily housed, with actors coming somewhere in between. I was very often present at evening meals or evenings at the vicarage.

The church was one of my absorbing interests in London. An Anglo-Catholic, I had, in my Princeton days, been an avid reader of *The Church Times*, then an admirably edited periodical of the party. I used to relish the advertisements in the *Times* of clerical openings, always specifying, according to the code of the party, the exact grade of churchmanship, the degree of highness to which the vacant parish had attained. This was sometimes indicated by "white linen vestments," by "colored vestments," or, again, it might be by such a term as "Central Churchman preferred" or "Moderate high," or by the number of late celebrations: "first and third Sunday of each month," or by the distinction between Eucharist and mass. The plenary badge reserved for the very highest was "full Catholic privileges," which meant late mass every Sunday, fasting Communion, auricular confession, reservation of the Blessed Sacrament.

In *The Church Times* I had read of all the celebrated Anglo-Catholic parishes in London; and ordinarily I "got in" every Sunday one and sometimes two of them—All Saints, Margaret Street; St. Alban's, Holborn; St. Mary's, Graham Street; St. Mary the Virgin's, Primrose Hill; St. Magnus the Martyr, mentioned in *The Waste Land*. Sometimes I went to one of the famous Roman Catholic churches, like that of the Farm St. Jesuits, or the very elegant church in Spanish Place; and I was amused to find that the ceremonial and decor in the papal churches of England were often less florid and Italianate than that of Anglo-Catholic churches. The Roman churches seemed more Anglican, as though to convince the Englishman that he need have no further fear of ultramontane domination.

My interests were heartily ecumenical. One Sunday in London I got all three "branches" of the Catholic Church (as Anglo-Catholics reckon things) into one morning. I made my Communion at eight o'clock at the Anglican Church of St. George's, Bloomsbury, just around the corner from my hotel; I then went to the Spanish Place Roman Catholic church for a nine-thirty mass; and I concluded with the Divine Liturgy at the Russian Orthodox cathedral. The effect was one of exhausting exhilaration.

In London, where I spent most of the year, it was my habit to work, ordinarily for five hours daily, at the British Museum, just around the corner from my hotel. Its center was a great Reading Room, surmounted by a dome. Since the interior had never been repainted since the museum was built—early in the nineteenth century, the names of the British authors which, in gilded lettering, surrounded the dome were outmoded, a period piece, the eighteenth century's choice of the classic. Chaucer and Shakespeare did not appear on it, but Addison, Pope, and Gibbon did.

The Reading Room is a museum of persons as well as books.

A reader has to have some kind of certification to be given a card of admittance; you can go on working, reading, or just lingering there, as long as you live. The population of the British Museum included both the most eminent scholars I had ever heard of but also, as well, many strange characters, not only poverty stricken but almost illiterate, who came to pass their winter days in a heated room.

No books may be removed from the library. Books must be read in the library. But they can be indefinitely reserved for a reader from day to day. And each reader's desk has slips containing his name inserted in the reserved books, so that, walking through the Reading Room, one can identify the readers: known, unknown, to be known, never to be known. So I was able to recognize the Reverend Montague Summers, a gross fat priest—whether Anglican, Roman, or defrocked, it is impossible to say—who had edited Restoration dramatists, written a loosely constructed book on the Gothic novel, and was an authority on demonology, black magic, and witchcraft, in all of which he was a believer. I was able also to identify the learned Jesuit, Father Herbert Thurston, a scholar whose name did honor to his order. But in the room with these and other learned persons sat an elderly Negro, whose reserved reading every day was an elementary arithmetic and the King James Bible, and an elderly lady who spent her days writing innumerable letters on ruled stationery.

The museum has a right to a free copy of every book published in England, but it is rich also in special bequeathed collections, so that there is scarcely a book, English or American, which it is impossible to find there. This richness was a temptation. Ostensibly, I was in England to write a book on the seventeenth-century poet Crashaw; but what scholars call "the wealth of material" was too much for me to resist. I read not only everything about Crashaw and Crashaw's contemporaries, but widely in books on mysticism and poetry, making my own anthology of extracts from rare books, which, had it been published, would have been something like Aldous Huxley's *The Perennial Philosophy.*

It used to be my habit to work on two or three books at once. During the year at the British Museum I got nothing written on Crashaw, though I filled volumes with notes. But I was still interested in Pope, on whom I had published my book the year before, and I was halfway through the composition of a second book, an intellectual biography of the elder Henry James. In consequence, I read widely in the rare Swedenborgian books as well as in the

Catholic mystics. I published several articles on Pope drawn from my studies in the museum, one of which agreeably necessitated my using the original manuscript of Pope's *Odyssey*, preserved in the Rare Book Room. Since paper-saving Pope had written his translation on the back of folded letters, I had the fun of reading his correspondence as well as examining the rough drafts of the translation.

At Oxford, I worked in the beautiful Reading Room of the Bodleian Library, with the original painted ceilings and woodwork of its founder's time, and with alcoves lined with rows of six- teenth- and seventeenth-century folios and quartos. In one such alcove, during some spring days, I read, in the original folio edition, *Psyche*, a religious epic by Crashaw's Peterhouse friend, Joseph Beaumont.

Oxford and Cambridge both delighted me, but especially Cam- bridge. At Oxford, I had a student friend at Worcester College and had the pleasure not only of eating with him in his chambers and hearing Chesterton at the Union, but of having breakfast with the delightful eccentric theologian, Canon Streeter. But at Cambridge I found a university far less encroached upon by the city; and there were not only the "backs" of the three great colleges to give me pleasure, but Peterhouse, Crashaw's own college, with its chapel built by the then master of the college, Dr. Cosin, and, adjoining Little St. Mary's, the fifteenth-century church of which Crashaw was curate for some time. I was delighted to find this church, surrounded by a garden of wildflowers, now possessed by the An- glo-Catholics, and served by priests with a ceremonial which would greatly have pleased Crashaw, as it did me.

In London I attended many concerts, notably those at Queen's Hall. I also heard Arnold Dolmetsch and his family give one of their concerts on clavichord, viola da gamba and other instruments of the baroque period. Their performance was not, as a musical performance, very satisfactory. There was something antiquarian about it, as, indeed, there might be, since Dolmetsch had con- structed these instruments himself after centuries of their disuse. An enthusiast for the seventeenth- and eighteenth-century arts, now called baroque, I was more touched and edified by the vener- able dignity of Dolmetsch and the family's loyalty to their cause and mine, than I was aesthetically gratified by the sounds pro- duced: mostly pipings and feeble grunts.

When I went to London in 1930 I was not a "literary man": I had known no poets or critics, only literary scholars, a few of them men of rare sensibility, like Joseph Beach at Minnesota and Morris Croll at Princeton. However, my elementary interest in poetry led me to visit Harold Munro's Poetry Workshop, near the museum. I bought a few contemporary books at his shop. The shop sponsored a series of weekly readings given by poets from their own work, and those I attended rather often, hearing and seeing the silver-bearded classical poet, Sturge Moore, and Sir Osbert Sitwell, highly gifted writer of poetry, short stories, novels, and most recently of a magnificent autobiography, one of the greatest in our literature. Sitwell was a very effective reader of his own early verse, which is less mannered than Dame Edith's of the same period, but shrewd, subtle, masterly.

My first personal acquaintance with a living poet was with T. S. Eliot. Though I had read some of Eliot's poetry, I neither understood nor approved of it, sharing in those days the views of Paul Elmer More, who admired, as I did, Eliot's "classical"criticism, but found his poetry obscure, incoherent, and Romantic and perhaps worst of all, inconsistent with the professed classicism of his essays.

I carried with me to London no letter of introduction to Eliot. I merely wrote him, who was the author of an essay on Crashaw, that I was in London working on Crashaw and would like to meet him. Eliot promptly replied and generously invited me to lunch. I must have mentioned my interest in the elder Henry James, a phrase which he probably misunderstood, for at lunch he talked about *The Ivory Tower* and *The Sense of the Past*, the two uncompleted novels of Henry James, neither of which I had read. Eliot no longer looked the Arrow collar advertisement youth of his early portraits. At forty, he wore spectacles, had lost some of his teeth, and was sallow of complexion. And if he no longer looked the young eagle, he did not look like a poet either: he was dressed in business clothes, wore a bowler, and carried a tightly furled umbrella—like any good London barrister. Eliot's manner was a combination of verbal precision with British urbanity. I can't forget the kindness with which he treated me, a gauche young American, who, though neither a poet nor an admirer of Eliot's own poetry, had sought his acquaintance.

Upon one call at Eliot's office, I met Mario Praz, then professor of Italian at the University of Liverpool, a brilliant scholar-critic and already the author of an Italian book on Crashaw and Donne. Eliot asked me whom else I would like to meet. I named "Evelyn Underhill," whose book on mysticism I had read. Eliot said he had not met her either, but promised to arrange a luncheon at which we both might do so. We met for such a meal at the London apartment of Mrs. Moore's cousin, Canon Underhill. Expecting to hear Eliot and Mrs. Moore talk profoundly on this occasion, even mystically, I had a lesson in the manners of well-bred poets and mystics, at least when they are also British, for no mention was made of these shared interests and nothing profound or even subtle was said. Eliot would ask of Mrs. Moore, or she of him, about some well-known but to the inquirer personally unknown person "Is he a nice person?" *Nice* apparently had, for my British acquaintance, the value of *sound* for my friend Bissell: it stood for everything one approved of, from breeding to morals and metaphysics. Later I was invited to tea with Mrs. Moore at her house in Camden Hill, and I found her the same gracious lady, but I had no sense that I was dealing with a mystic, and dared not presume to raise the topic.

Mr. Eliot was, as my grandmother would say, "a valued acquaintance," but I had friends nearer my own age, and station even more modest than mine. One of these was Frank Haskell, a working-class youth uncertain of his *h*s whom I met in Queen's Hall at an all-Stravinsky program conducted by the composer himself.

Frank, an avowed atheist, took me with him to a lecture by an old atheist, or positivist, in the nineteenth-century sense of the word. The lecturer was attacking the churches, but when the question period began it was clear that all the younger men present, including Frank, found that a dead issue—were more interested in the issue of communism versus capitalism.

A closer friend was Richard Carline, a painter, the son of a painter, and the grandson and great-grandson of painters. Dick lived with his old mother at Hampstead, near the Keats house. The walls of the house were filled—every inch of them—with the paintings of the past Victorian Carlines.

Dick's brother-in-law was Stanley Spencer, whose painting *"Resurrection Morning"* I had admired at the Tate Gallery. But Dick himself, who had studied at the Slade, the famous London art school which Ruskin had something to do with founding, had subsequently studied in Paris and was a talented postimpressionist. He took me to the Cafe Royal, the hangout of painters and writers; and he introduced me to many contemporary painters, both in the flesh and out of it. He gave me an initiation into the Bloomsbury equivalent in painting to the Eliotic taste in poetry.

London constantly excited me by its infinite variety. I loved it all, from Waterloo Bridge and the Thames embankment to Hyde Park and the Kensington Gardens. I never wearied of walking in London. There were always specificities to see, secondhand bookstores to visit, and pubs; but just walking the streets sufficed. Though I made excursions into the English countryside, into Surrey, the country did not compare, for me, with the city. I could heartily have concurred with Dr. Johnson: "He who is tired of London is tired of Life."

My delightful English year was delightably interrupted by a Christmas vacation, a fortnight long, which I spent in Paris and in the south of France. Two friends and contemporaries of mine, Johan Egilsrud (from my Minneapolis years) and Henry Grubbs (my regular dinner companion at Princeton) were both in Paris for the year, both working their five hours at the Bibliothèque Nationale. Johan was taking a Sorbonne doctorate, writing his dissertation on a genre already of interest to me, the dialogue of the dead; and Henry, already a Princeton doctor, with a dissertation on my favorite maximist, La Rochefoucauld, was enjoying such a fellowship as my own. Johan was living in the apartment of Mme. Masson, the mother of the painter André Masson; Henry, in a small hotel in Montparnasse, where he had already, by the time I reached Paris, found the best inexpensive restaurant, the best café for music, and the avant-garde cinema theaters. Both knew their way to the Dôme, where, innocently sipping Pernod, I sat for an appropriate length of time my first evening in Paris.

I was fortunate in my guides and educators: Johan, the elegant and charming dilettante, and Henry, a Princeton B.A. as well as Ph.D., very much the conscious man of the world, informed on every topic, as a scholar and a gentleman should be informed, yet without ostentation. Not quite "sound" in St. Peter's sense, for not quite serious, and more punctilious about details and general decorum than about more solid matters like religious and political faith, Henry was ever correct without rigidity or prissiness. Any analysis of such a kind would have been distasteful to him; but he would have silently conceded that I was the more creative, while I gladly yielded to and profited from his correctness.

The central scheme which prompted my crossing the Channel must have been Henry's. Under his guidance, we two made a carefully planned trip to the south of France—the careful planning, Henry's. It was to be, among other things, a "gastronomic pilgrimage"; and Henry carried along and diligently consulted his Michelin guide to restaurants. Three-star places were beyond our means; but for a place even to be listed in such a guide is a distinction. With unostentatious efficiency, Henry did all the work for us—booked our rooms at hotels, charted our course, bought our tickets. I had only to enjoy the scene, the food, the pleasures of travel, which, for me, are always considerable even if the travel is difficult: travel distracts my mind from its incessant and exhausting self-dissection.

Of our journey to Avignon, Nice, Marseilles, Aix-en-Provence, I have kept a long and detailed journal, not here to be reproduced— only to be made the subject of generalization.

The journal I wrote mostly in cafés—where I, as an American, was astounded to find I could sit all evening on the cost of a single café crème or a Pernod, the difficulty being to rouse the attention of an attendant if one wanted to repeat one's drink.

I have written at length about the Café de Paris, the principal café of Avignon, which we commonly visited for an apéritif before dinner at a hotel or restaurant, and where we generally spent several hours after dinner. In the evening, a trio—violinist, cellist, pianist—played, their permanent repertory, semiclassic to classic, listed on one available sheet. The atmosphere was that of a club, with its habitués whom I came to recognize. A white-bearded old gentleman in pince-nez read the *Revue des deux mondes*, vaguely an equivalent of our *Atlantic Monthly* as it used to be. Cultivated ladies wrote letters. A young man appeared to be writing, or revising, his poems. A few small groups played cards. And the music was really good. Later, in Paris, Henry took me to a similar *café concert* which he frequented. This was in 1930. I wonder whether such indoor cafés still exist, complete with music. Certainly the British intellectuals and artists, who had their Cafe Royal in London, deplored the general British absence of cafés; and a young American could immediately lament the absence of such from his own scene—whether the indoor public club, as one might call it, or the out-of-doors sidewalk cafés, where one can pause, rest, reconnoiter, and observe the world.

There is much in my journal of Provence and Paris about food. Henry was the daring explorer, who ate roast lark and snails; but I took to bouillabaisse at Marseilles and regularly, and with pleasure, ate meat. "I have acquired," I wrote, "many correct habits of eating and drinking, and now know better than to call all alcohol drinks liquor; know the difference between the apéritif, the white wine (with fish), the red wine (with meat), the liqueur (after the meal), I know the order of the courses—hors d'oeuvre, soup, fish, entrée, salad, 'sweet,' cheese, 'dessert' (fruit), coffee. I know that the French don't smoke during their meal, and certainly not before their soup." And many menus I give in detail. The introduction to the French cuisine which Henry imparted showed me that cooking could be an art and eating a cultivated pleasure, to be taken seriously.

It was the sense of civilization which France most gave me, and the need of a sensuous, not merely an intellectual, abstract, bookish culture—those things, and a desire for the past, for antiquity. I wasn't merely interested in painting and architecture. I was really converted by Arles, and especially by the cloisters of St. Trophime, to the Romanesque style (which I now definitely preferred to the Gothic); yet it mattered more that I was passing some enraptured leisure in a world which went back, as Provence did, to Roman times, but which had added stratification on stratification all the way down to the present.

And the infinite variety of life. I preferred the Edwardian tone of Menton (or Mentone) to the gayer life of Nice or of Monte Carlo, both of which we also visited; but I remember more strongly the contrasts of Marseilles, where we both attended what Anglicans would call choral evensong at the nineteenth-century cathedral and thereafter walked the short street of the prostitutes, where each harlot sat in the doorway of her cottage waiting for sailors to book their evening engagements. Churches, museums, hotels, a walk by the waterfront of Marseilles, dinners, music: all seemed a panoramic vista of a richer, vastly more varied world than I had ever known. The moralistic in me was held in abeyance, in suspense of judgment; the sociological existed not as an extension of the moralistic but as an element, I should blush to say, of the picturesque, the aesthetic.

After our return to Paris, I spent Christmas Eve with Johan and Henry at Mme. Masson's apartment. In our evening clothes, we taxied at ten to the Church of St. Eustache for the midnight mass, which began at eleven. We left at one-thirty, while the faithful were still making their communions, and returned to the Massons' for the *réveillon*, an elaborate cold supper, ending up with rum, cream, and sugar served in the drawing room. The conversation was entirely in French; but, so warm was the feeling of the company, so intuitive, that I began to understand what was said— or to imagine that I did. I ventured a few responses in French, without embarrassment; but found myself (verbal as I am) unembarrassed at participating, for the most part, nonverbally in the spirit of the evening and the gathering.

On the thirteenth of January, I was back in London and at the White Hall, my small hotel—disheartened by both. "The perpetual fog, dark, grime; the depressing streets, the heavy English faces. . . .," I wrote. I sorely missed Johan and Henry; still more, the gaiety and verve of Paris. But these feelings soon passed.

As the summer of 1931 came to an end, I faced the return to my native land, while Benny stayed behind, and, some years later, became a British citizen as well as a vicar. I remember wishing I could remain in England: would have had no compunction, at least then, about expatriation. But, since I had no notion how to manage to support myself, the idea of remaining never became definite, and the thought of returning to Boston attenuated the distress of returning to the United States.

The thought of returning also to Boston University did not disturb me. When my year off from teaching began, I remember wondering how I would, and whether I could, manage a frame of existence for myself—without a schedule prescribed by an institution; whether I could work regularly at what I set for myself to do. It was a permanent relief from this worry about my own self-sufficiency to find that I could.

I was not dismayed at resuming a schedule set by others when I was assured that I could devise a life for myself as well; and the chief benefit of a year of self-set work and self-chosen attachments and divertissements was made evident in the eight years which followed.

8

Boston: A Yankee Apartment in an Ethnic City

My mother and my grandmother Dillingham had both died within a few months of each other not long before I left for my year in London. Upon my return, in September 1931, I was greeted at the Cunard wharf in East Boston by my father, from whom I had, during the year, heard little. After an embrace and a kiss (for he was an affectionate man), he told me, with some embarrassment, that he had a surprise for me. Then from her position, at a little distance, he produced a plain and angular woman whom he introduced as about to become his wife. I learned later what my father had withheld from me during the year of my absence. Bewildered by the loss of his so much loved wife, and tormented by his loneliness, he had found his nights unendurable. After the evening milking of the cows, he had been in the habit of driving to Ashburnham, for him a kind of holy place, coming back just in time for the morning milking. He did not need to remarry in order to have either a cook or a housekeeper: at the function of both, he excelled either of his wives. But he did need a companion, someone who needed him.

With my favorite grandmother dead and my father remarried, I couldn't "go home again." The Waltham world on Russell Street still survived intact. But that world was virtually self-sufficient; and, though I made reasonably frequent trips to Waltham, especially to see my aunt Etta, ever my grandmother Dillingham's only real rival in my affections, I had now to make a world for myself, and—even though I had returned to Boston University—to make an almost entirely new world. London had liberated me: I returned with a new confidence in myself and a considerably clarified notion of what I wanted to do and, especially, to be.

Thus far I had contented myself with a rented "room of my own"; had not aspired to a house or even what the British call a flat and we Americans an apartment. How the ambition to rent an apartment rose I don't remember; nor do I remember how I thought of renting one on Beacon Hill. This hill, at the front of which stands Bulfinch's gilded statehouse, comprises two disjunct worlds. The front side, the side which rises from Boston Common, is the town seat of the aristocracy or the gentry: Beacon and Mount Vernon and Chestnut Streets with their auxiliary smaller companions, with Louisburg Square, Boston's fine replica of some London squares. But there is a back side, which slopes sharply from Revere Street down to Cambridge Street: the streets on this side are humbler. They are bordered now partly by tenement houses, partly by small brick houses, four stories high, which open directly onto the sidewalk, modest houses with but two rooms on a floor, yet with some good architecture.

This whole area had, in the later nineteenth century, become, as Howells's *An Imperative Duty* testifies, a Negro quarter. By 1931, the convenience of location and the really modestly good chaste architecture of the small brick houses, had turned the area into Boston's closest equivalent to Greenwich Village—a world for poets, artists, and other emancipated folk who bought up and partially restored the small houses to occupy themselves or rent. But the conversion of these streets into a Bohemia, or the coast of it, was uncompleted when I moved to the Hill. Across the street from me was a large tenement house occupied by Italians and a few Negroes. Just around the corner was an Orthodox synagogue: the elderly men, bearded and dressed in their long black coats, were a familiar sight on the street. So, though less frequent, were the matrons in their wigs, the honorable sign of the marriage state. There was a small Jewish grocery store just opposite the synagogue.

I first occupied the fourth, the top, floor of one brick house on Garden Street, and then, after a year, moved to a duplex occupying the third and fourth floors of another house, a few doors down. Here, where I lived for some years, I had an apartment admirably suited to my bachelor needs. On my upper floor were two small bedrooms; on the lower floor, a "drawing room" at the front, with my small study (which must originally have been a small bedroom) adjoining it; behind the front room, a back room which served as a dining room as well as kitchen (the stove, sink, and set tubs were ceremonially hidden by a low folding wall) and even music room, for it eventually contained a sizable French harmonium, or reed organ, a Mustel, made in Paris in 1880, and enclosed in a rosewood case, brass-handled, shaped like a sarcophagus.

Except for my aunt Etta, who had cherished a Chippendale chair and a Windsor, the latter still preserving its proper bottle green, and a secretary, which had been her grandfather's, none of my family on either side had any interest in antiques or taste for them—nor, more generally, any real interest in furniture or how to arrange it, in decor or interior decoration. In my mother's later years, and my grandmother's, I was more or less trusted to arrange the rooms. My instinctive confidence that I knew tables and chairs as well as the fine arts, my confidence that my aestheticism went beyond them into the application of art to the environment of daily living, came to me gradually over my teens and twenties. Many persons whom I admired for their intellects, or even for their taste in literature, cared neither about their dress nor their setting, background, visual context—concerns which I felt, and thought, should be an extension of their more specialized distinctions.

During my years of renting rooms, I had carried with me my *lares* and *penates*, which included candlesticks and some sacred picture, some icon (to use the word, as I like to do, in something larger than its technical sense); and I had rearranged the provided furniture as best I could to take psychic possession of the rooms. But now I had what I felt to be an establishment, a house of my own (I never owned a house till late in life, nor ever really wanted to: as a "stranger and a pilgrim" in this world, I felt that better symbolized my state). Now I had, and delighted to have, the responsibility to collect and arrange a setting for myself; and I found myself already in possession, without ever elaborately formulating it, of what Poe calls a "philosophy of furniture" and conception (his word again) of "keeping."

I lacked both the money and the ambition and even the desire to set up an establishment equipped with the classic urban furniture of the eighteenth century, of Chippendale and Sheraton. My taste was for Regency and Empire—for what, in America, were the Federal and early Victorian, the Civil War, periods. The light and cheerful woods, maple and pine, were not for me: I wanted rosewood, mahogany, even black walnut—the somber and solid and massive and, for their period, the grand and the elegant.

I do not like sitting rooms and even less living rooms; like neither the words nor the realities they connotatively invoke. I wanted to set up a drawing room and, more generally, an establishment, such as I should have had behind me as a family background—should have had but didn't. I wanted, as myself a partial archaism, to reconstitute a "visible past," that of grandparents and great-grandparents—to give myself the repose and fixity of a less hurried and more dignified urban New England.

My Beacon Hill apartment, with its small, low-ceilinged rooms, could not accommodate large, heavy, and high pieces—the black walnut secretary and the marble-topped sideboard which I had been given when the Auburndale house was dismantled; so it was the intimate and elegant at which I had to aim, with which I was content.

I did not attempt to reproduce any single drawing room recollected, nor study to make everything of a single period. I trusted my taste to choose what went together. But there was, I remember, a distinct desire to create a room my grandmother Dillingham should have wanted to have, and could have had—a room with pieces from 1830 to 1880 —nothing later.

I like to think of the sources upon which I drew. From my grandmother Dillingham's stock came a favorite walnut table of the spool work current at the period of the Civil War and also, and choice, a small mahogany table with twisted spiral legs and fine glass knobs, found after my grandmother's death in the maid's room at the Oak Bluffs summer cottage. From my father's farmhouse came a sleigh bed (which I had slept in during my last years at home) and a spool bed. And my father provided me with a dozen or fifteen of the bushel boxes in which he used to ship his apples to Boston. Walnut-stained, as he gave them to me, they made admirable housing for not-too-large books; and they could be built up into sectional cases, into sundry architectural formations.

Then my old Wesleyan and St. Peter's friend, Benny Bissell, had family furniture stored at Hebron; and from this store he generously gave me three mahogany side chairs (with slip seats upholstered in black horsehair, which I replaced by velour), an eighteenth-century candlestand, and an early tavern table, then painted green.

These were my inheritances. For the rest I purchased, from the antique shops which lined Charles Street at the foot of the Hill, but even more from the Morgan Memorial, the first of the Goodwill stores, founded by a Boston Methodist minister. The Boston shop, across the railroad tracks in the West End, dealt both in secondhand furniture and in books; and, in 1930, when many families were giving up their large houses and when young people had no taste for nineteenth-century furniture, the Morgan Memorial was a good place to buy both. From this source came my two excellent black walnut armchairs, which friends have supposed must have been my grandmother's, also a fine walnut chest of drawers with curved top drawer and gracefully curved front legs. The love seat, of the same period as the chairs, might have turned up at the same hospitable source, but it actually came from Charles Street, as did the ottoman.

Most of the furniture I acquired had to be reupholstered and refinished. It was the late-nineteenth-century habit to freshen up old furniture by applying a new coat of paint or another layer of varnish: my grandfather Dillingham was fond of painting and varnishing; and so were the old men whom the Morgan Memorial employed to put into salable shape the donated furniture. I spent what was for me a good deal of money having a Scotch craftsman I had discovered scrape off paint and apply sandpaper. This was done with proper advantage to most of my pieces; but occasionally, as in the case of the tavern table, I thus unpainted a piece which, in its period (as in the case of Windsor chairs and most Hitchcock chairs) had originally been painted. The zeal of the restorer had "eaten me up."

Some articles early acquired have still escaped my mention— notably a Pembroke table of peg construction with handsome tapering legs, which has long served me as my writing table, and a mantel clock in the French style of the 1880s—a brass-framed clock, the pendulum visible through its glass case, which sounds the hour and half hour in a dim musical chime.

My apartment offered no easy chairs of any kind, nothing overstuffed or padded. There was no provision for lounging or sprawling. A word neither in my vocabulary, nor in my system, was *relax*. For myself, I liked a stiff-backed chair. Reading, writing, or conversing, I was all at attention. This tenseness made rest in the horizontal position from time to time necessary; in my thirties, I took a nap late in the afternoon when I returned from teaching; and in lying down I could also meditate. But otherwise I sat stiffly: I read, pencil in hand, at my desk; or read, and sometimes wrote, standing up, after the mode of nineteenth-century authors—a very good mode. For a few years, I owned a standing desk, provided by Morgan Memorial, but the top of a chest of drawers would serve me as well.

On the drawing room floor were three small but good oriental rugs. The best, a Persian, had been left me by my great-grandmother Butler, who had never used it on the floor but had placed it against the back of some settee. The pictures on the walls were in gilt frames or black walnut. Like my father, I delighted to pick up frames and make my own insertions. In my back room, I had two original Currier and Ives prints, already provided with black walnut frames. In the front room hung a fine engraving of King Charles I and his family, and some oils by a Boston painter who summered at Provincetown, where I bought his landscapes, vaguely reminiscent of Cezanne. Into an oval walnut frame, the kind celebrated by Poe in one of his tales, I had inserted a lithograph portrait of an elegant Boston dilettante whom I had known in his handsome old age, when he resembled *der alte* Browning: in this, his youthful visage, the resemblance was to the familiar picture of *der junge* Hawthorne. This picture I liked to think of as an ancestral portrait—of some aesthetic uncle, perhaps. It was the only "family picture" to be seen.

The chief treasure on my walls was, however, a Russian icon of moderate size, a version of the traditional Eastern Orthodox icon representing the descent of Christ into Hades to awaken the Old Testament saints from their slumber. This, bought at Tiflis, in the Caucasus, had been given me by the French woman who had acquired it. As a newspaper correspondent, she had visited Russia just after the Revolution, when such sacred objects were exposed for sale in the marketplace; and, deeming me worthy, she gave it to me.

My early partiality for candlesticks, a partiality with ecclesiastical overtones, continued. How many pairs Garden Street exhibited I don't remember: but it was at this time, and soon after the munificent gift of the icon, that I acquired, from a Charles Street antique shop, a pair of prerevolutionary Russian candlesticks brought to Boston by émigrés. These were my choicest possessions in kind.

From my grandmother's stock, partly inherited from her mother and her stepmother, I inherited dishes and silver. For ordinary use, I bought Japanese-made blue willow ware such as then, and for some time to come, could be bought at Woolworth's; otherwise I needed no supplements. By mutual arrangement, my grandmother's Haviland dinner set went to my brother and his wife; I chose the two incomplete sets of old white and gold china, suitable for afternoon tea. Of silver I had an abundance: two tea services—one, delicate; one, large and heavy, equipped with coffee and chocolate pots as well. The knives, forks, and spoons were of sundry styles, and included some coin silver spoons sold to my Methodist forebears by adherents to the Millerite Adventist heresy who disposed of their worldly goods before, one day in the 1840s, they mounted the nearest hill ready to greet their returning Savior.

At Garden Street I attempted no full-scale housekeeping. I got my own breakfast and, if at home, my lunch, but always dined out—which could be done easily, inexpensively, and well on the Hill. Especially during the depression, there were many small neighborhood restaurants run by quasi artists, Bohemian young couples.

My dishes were washed, my beds were made, and my rooms kept in order by my "family retainer," a dainty elderly mulatto woman, Mrs. Thomas, who lived just across the street and came in daily. During the years of Prohibition, she brought me, concealed under her coat, bottles of red table wine made by her Italian neighbors. When I gave teas, which I did with fair frequency, she wore a black dress with a lace-bordered white apron, a gold cross on a chain round her neck (for she was a Catholic). I was proud of her as an ornament to my establishment. Once when I was on a vacation, and fastidious friends occupied my apartment, they discovered that this dainty woman was, to speak more gently than they did, a sloppy housekeeper: the set tubs were bug infested, and dirt had been swept under the rugs. These revelations rather amused than shocked me: they did not diminish my elderly handmaiden's picturesqueness and charm.

My apartment was at a location ideal for one who, unable to drive a car, must live within walking distance of the necessities of life—for me to be defined as churches, libraries, classrooms, and restaurants. Garden Street, on the back side of the Hill, offered indeed much more than the bare essentials. Louisburg Square and Scollay Square were within easy reach, and are offered here as making a polar pair of the genteel and the crude, a necessary balance. I could climb up Garden Street to the top and go down the "proper" side to Mount Vernon Street and then to Beacon Street past the gold-domed statehouse and so down to Boston Common, to Tremont Street past King's Chapel and on to the book boxes outside Goodspeed's bookshop under the Old South Church. Or I

could go down Garden Street, along Cambridge Street and Charles
Street, past the antique shops, to the Anglo-Catholic Church of the
Advent, where I attended mass, and beyond that to the esplanade.
Or I could walk to the public gardens and through them, to Copley
Square—to Trinity Church and to the public library just across the
square.

I shall now, however, go back to my apartment and set out,
in the opposite direction, for Scollay Square, down Cambridge
Street past Asher Benjamin's admirable West Church, where Dr.
Cyrus Bartol, one of the last generation of transcendental Unitarians, used to preach. At Scollay Square I could stop, as I often did,
for a beer, or I could take in a movie or see a few acts of superior
vaudeville at Loew's Orpheum, or I could cross the square and go
down Cornhill to the secondhand bookshops or down Hanover to
the Italian North End, at which (after my first visit to Italy) I could
see and smell and, if I chose, eat something of "Europe."

The North End delighted me, in its mixture of old New England and old Europe. It was the most ancient part of Boston. Here
stood, on Hanover Street, a handsome brick church, now St.
Stephen's Roman Catholic, which had been built as the Second
Congregational Church, on the site of a yet older one of which
Cotton Mather and Ralph Waldo Emerson had been, in their time,
the ministers. A little farther, one came upon Christ Church, the
Old North, a fine edifice in the eighteenth-century meetinghouse
style, with a three-decker pulpit at the east end, while in a gallery
over the entrance door, stood the oldest organ in Boston, splendid
of *buffet*, surmounted by mitre and crown. I had seen, I thought,
among Wren's London churches, none finer or more tastefully restored, than the Old North and King's Chapel in my own city. The
Old North, a prerevolutionary Anglican church, and still Episcopal,
held Sunday morning service, which I sometimes attended, chiefly
for the sake of the chaste neoclassical interior and the rich sound
of the unmodernized organ; but it now had no resident congregation: for its neighbors, the Episcopal church had built, next door,
a small brick chapel for Italian converts, whom I would suppose
to have been few. A more sensible construction, presumably contributed by the city, was a brick-walled and brick-paved courtyard
from which was to be had the best view of the Old North, especially of its apse; and in this courtyard, modeled on Old World
analogies, old Italian women knitted, all through the summer, and
old male Italians played.

Just a few steps of a steep ascent up from the front door of the

Old North brought me to Copps' Hill burying ground, the oldest of the Puritan cemeteries, from which one had a fine sweeping view of Boston Harbor. This yard was furnished with slate gravestones except for a few table tombs, in one of which was buried Dr. Cotton Mather, early a flawed hero of mine. The combination of the slate stones, with their crude iconology and their half-effaced inscriptions, and the ocean, symbolic of mortality and eternity, invited to meditation; and my quiet pleasure was enhanced if an Italian family seated on one of the table tombs lunched undisturbed.

The whole ethnic mixture of Boston was much to my taste. I was, in the early 1930s, to become drawn to the Greeks and the Armenians and their churches. From my twenties, I had paid visits to Negro churches. My students at Boston University were chiefly Irish and Jewish; I found the Jewish girls often brilliant; and I was then, and thereafter, throughout my career as a teacher, more intelligible to the Jews and Irish than to my fellow Yankees—the New Englanders of English stock, of whom I came, and among whom I had been reared.

So I gradually began to find, in the early 1930s, an office, a role which I could perform—that of interpreting the Yankee New England to the newcomers, many of whom, especially the Irish—who, having come to Boston in the 1840s, and who, having since the late nineteenth century ruled Boston politically—thought of themselves (not unnaturally) as New Englanders. As a Catholic-minded Episcopalian, a musician, and a literary man, I felt that I could enter into the world of Ireland. But I found it difficult to make attractive to my Irish students the virtues of either the higher or the lower species of Yankee: either the ethos of Jonathan Edwards, the Protestant scholastic philosopher, or of his classic Yankee antithesis, the practical Benjamin Franklin.

With the Jews, the case was different. As James Russell Lowell and Edmund Wilson have pointed out before me, the Yankees and the Jews (in both their higher and lower registers) have much in common—on the lower level, shrewdness, fondness for bargaining (or "swapping"), thrift, and practicality, and on the higher level, art, scholarship, intellectual disinterestedness, and sense of mission. Cotton Mather's *Magnalia* shows how constantly the parallels between Old Testament history and heroes and those of New England were invoked; and Justice Holmes found his chief disciples in young Jews such as Brandeis and Frankfurter.

The word *ethnic* was unfamiliar to me in the 1930s, but I had a strong feeling for the concept. I lacked any desire for an homogenized America. The richness of an ideal America, I thought, lay not in the suppression of ethnic or regional differences but in their preservation. The ideal America would be an international community founded upon mutual respect on the part of each contributing culture. In the 1930s, I was reading with deep sympathy the poetry of Gerard Manley Hopkins, so insistent on particularity as the counterpoint and balance to shared universals, and the doctrinal writings of Chesterton, from whom I derived the same impulse. Let us juxtapose but not blend—still less, blur or smudge our diversities.

If occasionally, then or thereafter, I fancied myself to desire the ethnic purity of a no longer extent Yankee village existing in isolation from alien peoples and cultures, I mostly knew better. What I really desired was what I already had, a Yankee apartment in the midst of a large and variously ethnic city.

9

Becoming a Professor

Living in Boston, and teaching at Boston University, I was soon given charge of the American literature survey course at my college. I had never *taken* such a course: none was offered either at Wesleyan or in the Graduate School at Princeton.

American literature as such or in its totality, was never my concern. I was not in my youth, and have never become, much of an "American." The country as a whole is too vast and too differentiated for my imagination or my loyalty to take in. I find it a programmatic abstraction rather than an organism—a kind of United Nations. I am a regionalist, a New England regionalist; and, when, actually or in my imagination, I leave my native region, I pass from it to England, "our old home," as Hawthorne, another New England regionalist, called it, and from England to Europe—which, for me, means France and (as for all American aspirants to culture) especially Italy.

As a teacher of American literature, I did my best to enter into, to empathize, Cooper and Poe and even Mark Twain; but, happily for me, most of classical American literature was written by New Englanders, if not (as Barrett Wendell is supposed to have supposed in his *Literary History of America*), by graduates of Harvard College. When the *New England Quarterly* was founded, by Harvard professors, at the end of the 1920s (a quarterly on the editorial board of which I served for two terms), it stretched the concept of New England to include Melville and Henry and William James. New England thus stood for the "paleface," "the egghead," and highbrow intellectual and the transcendentalist and symbolist line in America—a concept which I found entirely satisfactory. The prime New England writers for me were those polar figures, Hawthorne (whose *Works,* in the Riverside edition, my great-grandmother Butler had bequeathed to me), and Emerson. Of Emerson I could never arrive at a fixed estimate: in my Harvard course with Babbitt, I wrote a term paper attacking him as a Romantic and as anti-Christian—a position which later I could neither abjure nor wholly maintain. Emerson, lithe, sinuous, flexible, never ceased, never has ceased, to fascinate me, and to remain a fixed if elusive point of reference by which I could, at any time, estimate my own position. To Hawthorne I was less equivocally drawn. He was the regionalist, the conservative, the latter-day orthodox Christian who gave mythic form to the ancestral position; he was also the practitioner (as Henry James said) of the "deeper psychology."

I had begun to teach "American literature" and to write on New England authors during my first years at Boston University. Two essays on Bronson Alcott, one on his philosophy, intended as introduction to a small book collecting his *Orphic Sayings,* and another on *his* St. Peter's School—the Concord School of Philosophy, which ran for the summers between 1879 and 1887—were written before my year in London; the latter, based upon the regular reports of the lectures which appeared in the Boston newspapers of the period, was published in the *New England Quarterly* in 1929. An article, "Lowell on Thoreau," belongs to the same period. Transcendentalism was my first concern with American culture. Had I lived in the 1840s, I imagine that I, too, would have been a transcendentalist—unless, of course, I had become a neo-Calvinist, a belated Edwardian.

After I returned to Boston from London, I went on with my New England studies, publishing a selection from Hawthorne's sketches and tales in 1934. It was in preparation for writing my introduction to this book, which appeared in Harry Clark's American Writers Series, that I first began to read the American Puritans, especially Cotton Mather. But my veneration for the great Puritan-Calvinist Jonathan Edwards went back at least as far as Princeton days, for I remember then seeking out President Edwards's grave, which stood just off the campus. At Boston University, my lectures on Edwards were regarded by some of my students as among my best. Especially, they delighted to hear me perform the famous sermon, "Sinners in the Hands of an Angry God"—which I tried to read, not with all the orotundity and melodrama of which my voice and I were capable, but as dryly and quietly as Edwards is reported to have read his pulpit discourses. My private favorite among the Edwards selections in our survey anthology was, however, not the sermon but the "Personal Narrative," his account of his early mystical experiences.

Throughout my remaining eight years at the College of Practical Arts, I continued to teach a section or two of Freshman Composition. One text was a handbook (by Norman Foerster), of which my special pleasure was in the appendix on "Common Errors," duly prescribed as an assignment. I used to enjoy "teaching the errors," especially the dangling participle (DP, as the corrector's pencil affectionately noted it on the margin of a faulty "theme"by a student). Unlike most English teachers, I liked to teach grammar, even elementary: for, apart from the idioms, which must just be memorized, the rest is simply applied logic. The other freshman text was always a book of essays—not literary or familiar essays, but articles on current controversial topics like socialism and divorce, challenging essays which were intended to stir up discussion and incite to heated rebuttals of the "advanced" views propounded. I cannot remember that with PAL girls these had much educative effect, but they gave the English teacher, in his then role of forum expositor of social topics, an opportunity to work out his own ideas with an immunity which the professor of sociology would not have had.

The long-range efficacy of Freshman Composition remained to me dubious. My ground of particular objection was that what we unavoidably gave the secretarially headed girls was an instruction purely cosmetic: we taught them, for the time being, to avoid errors in the agreement of subject and verb, dangling participles, and faulty reference, not to overuse adjectives like *interesting, fascinating,* and *marvelous* and not to use trite metaphors ("the trees stood like sentinels"); but we did not, could not, remake the nature to which such errors and such diction were appropriate. As to their slang, for several years I used to set them to making out lists of all the words and phrases they considered such, and to request them to define them in simple direct language. This was the period of "for crying out loud," "for crying down the kitchen sink," "the cat's pajamas": the picturesque ones were of this variety. All of them could be classified as praise ("swell"), dispraise ("lousy"), and surprise ("gee whiz"). It was curious how much old-fashioned slang, of my time or before it, turned up along with the occasional novelties. These collections were made for my own elementary but real linguistic interest, the same interest which prompted me, as a

youth back in Stow on vacation from Wesleyan, to gather up all
the archaic Yankee phrases and pronunciations I heard on the lips
of our oldest and most rustic neighbors. I had in mind no special
reformatory program, unless gently to suggest that, if the girls
were to use slang, they should use the newest and most inven-
tive—if they were able to distinguish.

Another routine course I gave throughout my Boston University years was the sophomore survey of English literature; and that
I thoroughly enjoyed teaching. *Beowulf to Thomas Hardy* was the
text. One bright strategy the former head of the department
adopted: when he found how difficult it was to interest the students in the early, difficult authors, including Chaucer and
Spenser, he turned the courses around and began with Hardy and
his contemporaries. I am dubious whether, except for English ma-
jors, the historical survey was efficacious; probably the later ap-
proach by way of types or understanding types—the analysis of
poems, short stories, and novels—would have more likelihood of
interesting practical-minded, very normal young women. But, the
pedagogic choice not being mine to make, I was glad indeed to
take advantage of the survey in giving me the opportunity for a
yearly "grand tour," a yearly review of the history of a rich literature, to be reminded of, to empathize, authors whom, and periods
which, I would never be empowered to teach in specialized
courses. Early in the 1930s, I began to find myself as a literary
critic. It is at least as necessary for the critic as for the poet to
have Eliot's "historical sense," the "feeling that the whole of the
literature of Europe from Homer and within it the whole of the
literature of his own country has a simultaneous existence." This
enforced yearly living through all the period styles of English, and
at least by implication European, literature was of steady value to
one who saw criticism as comparison.

My work at the College of Practical Arts fell into two groups—
the required courses and surveys, and the elective courses for a
small group of young women who had literary talents and aspirations. Of such, there were always twelve or fifteen juniors and
seniors, unofficial honors students, who were my special parishioners and disciples—always as many as, giving them individual attention, I could properly teach.

My offered elective, Creative Writing, I gave each year: it was
my special and characteristic class. The title I of course disliked:
creative is a pretentious word for "imaginative"; and, no more than
another who managed such a course, did I suppose that I could

create a creator. I could, as a literary critic and man of letters, help those who, hoping they had talent, wanted to write, by reading closely and critically what they wrote and by proposing approximate models among contemporary writers. Most of all, I could arrange that the aspirants had the mutual stimulation of meeting together, and I could provide them with time for writing by giving them academic credit for a course.

Writers are both born and made. There is talent; there is also craft. Most of the writers we know about have either gone without craft or have acquired it, as Hawthorne and Henry James did, by studying, analytically, the novelists of the preceding generation or two. As Sir Joshua Reynolds said in his *Discourses*, "The daily food and nourishment of the mind of an artist is found in the great works of his predecessors." This is as true of the writer as it is of the painter. But the writer has the advantage over the painter that he has much longer had the "museum without the walls"—printed books, to which he could have recourse whenever he would.

I have no wish to do away with models and imitations. As a matter either of acquiring literary culture or of learning to write, it is a good discipline to play "the sedulous ape." The normal way to grow is to imitate, and then in turn to reject or "transcend by including," a whole series of models. The poets who eventually arrive at what reviewers call a voice of their own commonly do so after an imitative first and sometimes second book. It is rare indeed that originality is crushed or thwarted by imitation; and probably when it is, the writer has no originality worth the cost of preserving.

Neither a creative writer nor a frustrate one, I have had my qualms about professing to teach creative writing. How can I teach what I can't do? To this I answer that those teachers who can do, almost unavoidably encourage others to do likewise, to perpetrate imitations of the master; and they judge these products by their approximation to the original, of which they hold the patent. As a critic, I might claim to command a wider spectrum of possible models and styles and kinds of excellence.

I would not undertake to defend courses in creative writing on the ground that many of the young writers of talent ever arrive at a professional status of importance. Talent, it would seem, is "to burn." What is needed is so much else, to which I should have to give the general name of *character*—ambition, persistence, singleness of purpose.

The defense of these courses, including my own, must be

mostly pedagogic. Anyone who is going to teach literature *as such,* not as a convenient compound of history and moral philosophy, ought to have had some experience of the practice of the art he is to teach, descriptively or critically. He ought to have some acquaintance with how the mind of a poet works. And he ought to give some space in his own life to self-expression, if only in that half-imaginative form of journal writing.

Throughout my career as a teacher, I have found the students who wanted to "write" to be also those who wanted to live—those who interested me as persons, personalities, individuals—those who are not merely receivers but givers. Perhaps this is the finally important reason for "creative" classes.

These existential spirits among the young women were my friends. There was already in existence when I arrived a Writers' Club; and its sponsorship was one of my most agreeable duties. At least once a semester, I entertained them at tea in my Hill apartment—occasions on which one of the elderly gentlewomen of my acquaintance often served as hostess, though the decorative and dainty Mrs. Catherine Thomas was well pleased, in the absence of such, to serve as the gracious *serva padrona.*

Of my originating was an annual anthology, clothbound, called *Varia,* which handsomely took the place of a college literary magazine. Somehow I succeeded in selling this book, an issue of which perhaps represented thirty-five contributors, to Dean Davis, who paid for it out of college funds. He presumably considered it a dignified advertisement, for it can scarcely have been of much interest to the "girls" except as the merest of mementos.

My other advanced courses at the college were chiefly directed toward fulfilling the needs as I saw them of these creative young. To approximately this group, I taught also a course in the modern novel which included Dostoyevsky, Proust, Mann's *Buddenbrooks* and the *Magic Mountain,* Gide's *Counterfeiters,* Joyce's *Dubliners* and *Ulysses,* Virginia Woolf, and Huxley's *Point Counterpoint.*

I offered, too, a course in Aesthetics and Criticism, which used as text the books of De Witt Parker and of David Prall and Parks's *The Great Critics.* As an amateur keyboard performer and choir director, I illustrated the musical part of the course by playing the piano as well as using the phonograph. The visual arts I had had far less opportunity to cultivate; but I was eager to learn and learned by teaching—primarily by taking my class to the Boston Museum to see the Japanese prints and screens, the Buddhist sculptures (the Boston Museum is rich in oriental art), the early Italian paintings, and the Copleys and Stuarts.

In addition to the practical aspects of this course, there was also the philosophical: it gave me opportunity to return to old favorite themes such as the relation of art to morality and the relation between art and ideas; and I made some beginning of exploring the meaning of meaning. An essay I wrote for the *Sewanee Review*, almost my earliest published venture into literary theory, took off from George Boas's *Primer for Critics* and I. A. Richards's *Philosophy of Rhetoric*.

The last course I began, in 1937, was devoted to the eighteenth century, the first literary period to interest me. This was open to graduate students as well as juniors and seniors; and, for the first time, I drew, to my seminar room at the college, a few men from the Graduate School, housed in the Liberal Arts College at Copley Square, where, for the last two or three years, I had taught the survey course in American literature. Also, for my last few years, I was a member of the all-university graduate committee and attended some oral examinations, though the chairman of that committee assigned to me the direction of no dissertations. During my Boston University days, I was, almost exclusively, a teacher of undergraduates and almost exclusively of women.

Yet, in those last few years, my reputation grew within the university. When the experimental two-year General College was founded, in 1937, with Dr. Edgar Brightman, the philosopher, the university's most distinguished single figure, as its sponsor, I was chosen to be its teacher of the humanities. And in the same year I was elected president of the Boston University Chapter of the American Association of University Professors, an organization which, in that then dispersed and scattered university, played an important local role in bringing together the intellectually alert and producing and publishing members of the faculty.

Though it was immediately connected with the college where I was professor, and with the creative writing class and the Writers Club, the latest of my projects went, in its scope and public recognition, beyond these parochial bounds. Dean Davis's applications to wealthy women had, in my last year in Boston, succeeded in winning the gift to our college of three buildings in Brookline. The donor, the widow of Larz Anderson, a former minister to Denmark, was, I think, an amateur poet. It must have been on some such plausible basis that I proposed to the dean, securing his assent, that one of the three buildings, a rather handsome, tile-roofed stucco house, be assigned to me for development of an Isabel Anderson Library of Poetry. In the spring 1939 issue of *Bostonia*, the alumni magazine of Boston University, appears a long statement, given out as from President Marsh but written by me, which, in six points describes both the "immediate objectives" of the library and yet more grandiose ultimate aims. Its first two aims were "the establishment of a collection of American, English, and French poetry, criticism, and aesthetics from 1900 on" and "the creation of a collection of the 'little magazines,' the patron-supported, laboratory magazines which, from 1900 on, have been the chief means of introducing new writers to the public."

The prospectus contains at least one fancy which I think I must have inserted to please sentimental ladies—as a kind of sentimental joke—"The creation, to the left of the Library, of a sunken garden, to contain all the flowers and flowering shrubs which have inspired poetry"; and another paragraph quaintly links together, as parts of a museum, "relics of the poets, including their manuscripts." There was to be a director's office on the first floor, which, the report says, "is being fitted with cabinets containing velvet-lined drawers for manuscripts"; and there were to be "studies or writing-rooms" on the second floor.

What was actually achieved in the spring and summer of 1939 was the collection and placement in the library of some six hundred volumes, all gifts solicited from their donors by my friend, the Boston poet John Brooks Wheelwright, whom I had named associate director. The donors included Mrs. Fiske Warren, the president for many years of the New England Poetry Society, Mrs. Irving Babbitt, Mrs. Ada Russell, the companion of Amy Lowell, and James Laughlin, the young publisher of New Directions. One of the most handsome gifts was a morocco-bound set of the *Hound and Horn*, from Stewart Mitchell, one of its editors.

The grander aim of the library was to create a sanctuary for poets. I am quoted by *Bostonia* as saying, "In America, . . . the values of the business man and the man of action take marked precedence over the contemplative values of the artist and the scholar." My real, if unrealistic and unrealized intent, was to give temporary support, in the form of fellowships for a year, or more permanent maintenance, to all the impoverished poets of ability with whom I was acquainted. Harvard had its Poetry Room; the University of Buffalo had, and I had visited, its collection of poets' work sheets and other manuscripts; Brown University had, and, again, I had visited, its Harris Collection of American Poetry, of which Wheelwright's brother-in-law, Foster Damon, himself a poet, was the directing spirit. It would have no doubt added luster to Boston University to have boasted analogous collections; but my motives were more far-reaching than I thought it wise to state.

The College of Practical Arts had come to an end: the assemblage of Boston University on a single campus abolished its pretext for being. But the books collected for the poetry center still exist as a separate unit of the university library, the Isabel Anderson Collection; and so there survives a modest, tangible relic of my labors in the service of Boston University.

10

Becoming a Guest

One of the fringe benefits of being an author is social recognition—
quite a different thing from acclaim by other authors—favorable
reviews, or honors, or friendships with one's peers. The social recognition given a writer is not by people who have necessarily read
him. It is given to him as a kind of eminence who at the same
time is reasonably presentable in dress and manners and is reasonably good company, a suitable dinner guest. The Boston of 1930
still possessed something like salons, presided over by mature
women with a taste for the arts and for personalities. They offered
civilized entertainment—teas or dinner parties. This was the world
I associated with Proust and Henry James—a world which, class-
conscious as I was, I had not really expected ever to be able to
enter.

But in 1934 the respectable trade publisher, Macmillan, published my critical biography of the philosophic theologian, the
elder Henry James. I had become interested in writing on him
through my long study of Swedenborg, whose disciple he professed
to be. It was, however, the fame of his sons, William the philosopher and Henry the novelist, which chiefly gave him attention
after his death, and which brought attention to my biography.
When I was writing it, I won the acquaintance and goodwill of
William's son Henry, the literary executor of the family papers,
and Ralph Barton Perry, of Harvard, William's editor and biogra-
pher, and I met and corresponded with other members of the James
family and their friends, both American and British.

The then Henry James—Henry II—apparently gave copies of
my book to his relatives, including his eccentric cousin, Edwin

Holton James of Concord; and through Edwin James, who invited me to his home in Concord, I met Rose Standish Nichols of 44 Mount Vernon Street, on the proper side of Beacon Hill.

Miss Nichols, in 1934 somewhere in her sixties (I never knew her exact age), became almost immediately my friend and well-wisher and social sponsor. I doubt that she ever read my *Elder Henry James* or any of my later writings, though I naturally provided her with copies. She was a reader neither of literature nor of philosophy—indeed, not much of a reader at all. Her memory was stocked with facts or supposed facts, the accuracy of which I never trusted; was filled with legends, traditional stories, and traditional gossip. She was apparently completely skeptical of the published or authoritative view of things: knew enough of the inner or behind-the-scenes view of persons and events not to credit anything which appeared in print.

Only gradually did I learn her own life story; I shall limit what I give of it to a few undisputed and verifiable facts. She claimed descent from the Standishes of Plymouth, Massachusetts. Her father was a physician, a general practitioner in Boston. Her uncle was the sculptor, Augustus St. Gaudens. A cousin was the once famous singer, Louise Homer. She was educated at a private day school; did not go to college.

Early in life she became interested in art and art criticism (she once showed me an early published essay of hers on Pater); and, with the need to earn her living she took up landscape gardening, under whose auspices or training I am ignorant. As long as I knew her, she made winter trips to Florida and California to give annual supervision to the gardens of wealthy women who had earlier commissioned her to lay them out. And she wrote and published at least three books on gardens, of which the first, *English Pleasure Gardens*, appeared in 1902, to be followed by books on French, Italian, and Spanish gardens. These books were based both on historical research and on visits to the gardens as they existed in her own time. The books give the impression of more scholarship and more intellect than, from our countless conversations, I would have supposed her to possess.

It is my impression that these artistic interests of hers belonged to her comparative youth; that they had, save for practical purposes of money earning, much receded by the time I knew her. The interests which had taken their place were mostly political. She was one of the founders of the Foreign Policy Association; and she followed diplomacy and high State Department affairs with keen interest. A strong liberal in domestic policy, an eager attender of the Ford Hall Forum, she was motivated, it would seem, by antagonism to the conservative and Republican world in which she was reared and in the midst of which she continued to live; for, in foreign affairs, she was predictably against whatever friends of her own class were likely to be for. In both world wars, she was— at least for argument's sake—on the German and Japanese side. Clearly, this was because most Bostonians—and most of all, her close friend from girlhood, Mrs. Fiske Warren—were Anglophiles, and she wanted to defend the underdog, even if ultimately indefensible.

She belonged with Jack Wheelwright among those complex characters who, aristocrats at birth, feel at once proud of their status and inheritance, yet rebellious against the stuffiness of their own class—a world into which I had no more than glimpses and would not have found more than ethnically interesting. No more than Jack could Miss Nichols endure being bored. So, while keeping a more-than-tolerated position in her own world, she sought the company of liberals and radicals, and of people in high places. She was fond of referring to "my friend, Queen Sophie" of Greece. She had known Mrs. Keppel, the distinguished mistress of King Edward VIII. In the years I knew her, she delighted in the company of retired admirals and other such dignitaries, who could tell her what "really" happened. Boston was too limited to serve as more than her fixed center and base. She often wrote me—and she was a copious though not a distinguished correspondent—from the Cosmopolitan Club in New York or the Cosmos Club in Washington—and sometimes from her club in London.

I have never known anyone who had known so many people eminent in one way or another: I never got to the end of her repertory of such memories. And it was one of the satisfactions and pleasures I gave her that my range of reading was versatile enough to enable me to follow, and appreciate, her repertory.

She must have been plain—or at least must have felt herself plain—in her youth, no match for the dazzling beauty and femininity of her friend Gretchen Warren: she was tall, angular, slim, her face possessed of a strong bone structure. In her old age, she was still so slim that she could wear—and occasionally did, to surprise me—a dress she had worn in her youth, along with a hat of the same period. She was in her old age handsome; but she can never have been pretty or girlish or attractive to marrying young men of her own age. She must always have been strong willed and strong-minded.

She never had money enough to claim automatic attention or deference on that ground. In terms of her own class, she was always poor. When I knew her, she lived on Mount Vernon Street; she owned a substantial brick house designed by Bulfinch, her family's; but the taxes on the house were heavy; and she had to scrimp and save in every way to manage to live. She could never afford a single competent woman servant to cook, clean, and open the door; sometimes she had an old crone; sometimes no one. She saved on food, and, of course, on dress.

Without wealth or beauty, or even obvious charm, how had she come to know everyone worth knowing—or whom at least, she cared to know? By virtue of what I most admired in her—an indomitable determination to live, and to be, and to be herself. She was certainly an intensely lonely person, but she allowed herself no self-pity—a vice as distasteful, as abhorrent, to her as to proud, lonely Jack Wheelwright. Nor did she allow herself fear: "forethought, not fear-thought" is a scrap of wisdom from the New Thought teacher Horace Fletcher which she sometimes used to quote to me. She was not a religious woman, even by the standards of Boston theistic Unitarianism, and not an Emersonian idealist; yet she was not worldly either, much as she liked to enjoy the luxury of other peoples' houses and motorcars. She was loyal to persons and causes, and (in Royce's phrase) "loyal to loyalty."

One thing which kept her alive and vivid was her relish for gossip. She abounded in mildly malicious anecdotes about her friends—or at least her acquaintances. Once when she took me to spend the afternoon with Ralph Adams Cram, the famous architect, a friend of hers from their youth, he playfully admonished her, "Rose, you should wash your mouth with iodine at least once a day." I, who never retail gossip, and who in consequence hear little of it, felt guilty at listening to Miss Nichols's anecdotes, yet felt it would be prim of me to attempt to stop her; felt, too, that I had no way of learning about the world except by overhearing what the world said—hearing how people talked, while remembering that what I was hearing was legend and fiction not sober history.

As she retailed gossip, Miss Nichols's face lit up and her lips parted, moist with the spittle of malice and fun. It was partly a kind of ugly adolescent's pleasure at meiosis, a bringing mighty adults low, at making fun of dignitaries and the self-important, and of the self-styled idealists and self-named beautiful souls—among the latest category, her lifelong friend, Gretchen Warren. It was partly a love of the picturesque—the kind that Bacon speaks of when he calls truth "a naked and open daylight that doeth not show the masques and mummeries and triumphs of the world half so stately and daintily as candle-lights."

Her well-known relish of gossip did not alienate my friend's friends; and the explanation lies in the loyalty she felt toward them. Had I, or anyone else outside the inner circle, have made fun of them, such an outsider would have been firmly put in his place. That Miss Nichols was fond of me, in her unsentimental way, I cannot doubt; and I was perhaps more an imagined nephew than a protégé. Had anyone else made fun of me—of my Anglo-Catholicism or any other foible or mannerism, I think she would have defended me.

She certainly wanted to help me, or my career, however I might define that, in any way she could. She saw me, I would think, as a gifted young man handicapped by the lack of a proper family and upbringing, who had, as such gifted young men often have, a desire to enter a larger and higher world than they were born into. She could not help me to get an appointment at Harvard, for which I am grateful: any meddling by women or other personal friends of one who might wish to rise academically can do little but damage the gifted outsider's chance. It must have crossed her mind that I might rise by making an advantageous marriage, for at least once she introduced me into a household with two marriageable daughters, ready for disposal. But I instinctively made it clear that I was not ready for marriage as a stepping-stone.

One thing she could do, she saw, was to teach me manners. I never forgot her rebuking me for tardiness in keeping an appointment; I, who still retained the feeling that an artist and a mystic was superior to punctuality. She reminded me how thoughtless of others this was—a thought which had not occurred to me. And she laid down as maxim and rule: "I wait five minutes for an acquaintance, ten minutes for a valued acquaintance, and fifteen minutes for a friend." I learned punctuality.

But the chief thing she could do was to introduce me to other cultivated women of mature years; and this she systematically proceeded to do. She hoped to give me other friends and other hostesses. She took me with her for lunch to the house of Mrs.

Ezra Thayer, who was an Anglican and a reader of Rilke in German; she took me to call on "Lily" Norton, daughter of Charles Eliot Norton, and named after Elizabeth Gaskell, the novelist—the icy and elegant Lily Norton, who divided her time between England and Beacon Street; she took me to lunch at the Republican Club to meet Mildred Howells, the daughter of the novelist; she took me with her to a weekend party at Mrs. Murray Crane's at Woods Hole, where I met Virgil Thomson, the composer.

Most of these introductions led nowhere. But two of them did. With Mrs. Fiske Warren of Mount Vernon Place, and Mrs. Kingsley Porter, of Elmwood, Cambridge, I established permanent relations.

Mrs. Warren lived almost around the corner from Miss Nichols, on Mount Vernon Place, a townhouse I came to know rather well. The dining room was in the basement. On the ground floor, there was a double drawing room running from front to back, the most conspicuous feature of which was a full-length portrait of Mrs. Warren, then an extraordinarily beautiful young woman, painted by Sargent. She is accompanied by her two young children, a girl and a boy, but they are accoutrements which do not engage her attention. At the top of the house was a ballroom, where I once attended a formal reception.

She was already in her lifetime a legendary figure. She was for three generations a Boston grande dame and hostess. She remained almost to the end a great beauty. I saw her but once after she had given in to age. But until then, she had spent time and money in keeping young and beautiful with the aid of all known methods of beautification. She meant, certainly, to be immortal, and nearly achieved it.

With her rather ageless than autumnal beauty—her slender figure, her delicate complexion, and blonde hair—she combined the spirit of a poet and a mystic. She had published two books of her poems, brought out (naturally) in England. She wrote in the manner of 1890–1910; like Gilbert Murray, she was vaguely Swinburnean, pre-Georgian. Her natural taste was for the Celtic twilight—for A. E. and the early Yeats, for poetry which sought to pass either into music or into vision, vision with nothing precise, sharp, or imagist about it.

She was not really an intellectual woman, though she may have seemed so to her friends. Indeed, she was not a discursive thinker at all, but highly intuitive, with powers, I concluded, of extrasensory perception. There were strange talks with her during which I deliberately suppressed thoughts as inappropriate, as I thought, to utter —only to find Mrs. Warren voicing them, apparently reading my mind and yet unaware that she was doing so. Certainly, whenever I saw her alone, what passed between us was much more communion than communication: it mattered little what was said; it was the "vibrations"that carried the relation.

Her taste in thought was naturally for the mystics and the mystical philosophers—among the latter, rather Plotinus than Plato—for Böhme and Swedenborg. When she opened each session of the New England Poetry Society, which regularly met in her drawing room for twenty years or more, she did so by reading aloud some "sacred texts" from the mystics and the mystical poets.

The best ideas of her favorite readings can be gathered from the anthology, *The City without Walls* (Macmillan, 1936), which her mother issued, with an introduction by the Irish poet A. E., an anthology which is a kind of ecumenical Bible. Mrs. Osgood, says A. E., has "ransacked the Scriptures, Christian, Buddhist, Brahmin, Chinese, Egyptian for their profundities and exaltations, and also a wide range of secular literature where it becomes half sacred because the intensity of the soul has burned away from time its dross, and there is a transparency through which there comes some transcendence up to Everlasting Light."

Most of what I know of Mrs. Warren's life derives from Rose Nichols, the plain friend of the highly feminine and at all ages beautiful Gretchen. Her maiden name, Osgood, was a sound Yankee name but without prestige. Hamilton Osgood, the father, called, whether legally or not, "Doctor," was a fashionable physician, a man of charm, especially for women patients. He had studied in Europe—in France, with Charcot, in Vienna also (though not, I believe, with Freud); was apparently some kind of psychiatrist, possessed of magnetism and much insight into the neurotic and semineurotic; was never regarded by Miss Nichols's father, a family doctor, as solid or even respectable in his attainments and practices.

He had married, in younger and poorer days, Margaret Cushing, the remarkable woman I knew in her extreme old age. During the struggling years when he was acquiring a practice, Mrs. Osgood ran a private school on the Hill. She was also a lieder singer—how professional I don't know, but she had an extraordinarily beautiful, low speaking voice, and, during the years I knew her, read lyrical poetry aloud with the studied placement of the voice, the phrasings and the pauses, of a trained singer: it was a delight to hear what in effect were recitals of poems; one such series, chiefly of pieces from the Irish Renascence, she recorded for Columbia.

The Osgoods married off both their daughters well—Margaret to Erskine Childers, an Englishman who espoused the cause of Irish freedom and died during the civil war; Gretchen, to Fiske Warren, a Bostonian of wealth. This marriage must certainly have required management to bring it off; it can never have been a happy or even congenial one; and the couple lived apart when I knew Mrs. Warren. The husband, whom I once met at a Social Credit meeting where he argued dryly for a rival theory, Henry George's Single Tax, has been described, by Bertrand Russell, as a "lean, ascetic, anxious character" with no time for "jokes or frivolities." He was a vegetarian and a teetotaler. He devoted all the money he could legitimately muster up to founding a Single Tax colony in Andorra.

So Gretchen Warren was left with her townhouse, her writing of poetry, her Poetry Society, her collection of seashells, in her converse with other fine spirits, one of them the learned, subtle philosopher Dr. Ananda Coomaraswami, curator of oriental antiquities at the Boston Museum, and such worldly friends as Eleanora Sears, the sportswoman. She found time also to launch her granddaughter into Boston society with a coming-out party at the Chilton Club. She took herself very seriously. She had a public image, which she carefully lived up to: that of the great lady, and that of the lover of Beauty: *Beauty*, with a capital letter clearly present in her enunciation, was probably her familiar, certainly her characteristic, word. She saw herself as a high priestess of culture in a world of falling standards, and the more rigidly the priestess as the world, even that of Boston, deteriorated. She, at least, had not relaxed her standards, either in poetry or in manners.

The sense of humor which Gretchen Warren lacked her mother richly possessed. She must, I suppose, have been ninety when I knew her; and she took delighted and picturesque pleasure in the license of her old age. According to Rose Nichols, she was not much noticed during her striking husband's life. She blossomed late. I can only think that the precarious finances, the managing of an amorous husband, and a beautiful and marriageable daughter, the general necessity for contrivance and for equilibrium among ups and downs and unpredictability must have helped her to her sense of the melodramatic and the grotesque. She had a vitality and earthiness which her so refined daughter either had never had or had purged off.

Mrs. Osgood was an actress, playing the part of an old, old lady and amused by her role. Sometimes she appeared to imagine herself an old Irish peasant woman, crooning over her hearth; at other times, she was a dowdy old lady, like Queen Victoria. Once when I rode with her in a cab bound for Cambridge, she wore a black bonnet, pushed back on her head. She was a Romantic and a "mystic" all right, but one with a sense of self-mockery along with the more properly mystical sense of how trivial and ridiculous all earthly conventions are. "We must treat this world as though it were real, though we know it is not." I paraphrase Emerson.

It was through Miss Rose Nichols again that I was introduced to Lucy Porter, the widow of Arthur Kingsley Porter, who had been professor of fine arts at Harvard, though Miss Nichols and she were but acquaintances. Mrs. Porter was not a Bostonian either by birth or lineage. She and her husband, both independently wealthy, whose money derived from fathers who were manufacturers, lived grandly indeed at Elmwood, in Cambridge.

Elmwood had been the home of James Russell Lowell, and of his clerical father before him. The basic structure of the house is the traditional New England white wooden house, foursquare, with a handsome central hall and staircase: a double parlor on the left of the entrance (the back parlor used by Lowell as his study and still shelving some of his books); at the right, the dining room, the room the Porters had done over. From their Italian sojourns they had brought back a dark refectory table and a credenza which served as buffet; and the walls of the dining room were hung with Italian paintings of early centuries, originals such as one saw in art museums. At the back of the house and to the left had been added a modern wing, a large room for receptions and concerts, which was used for Sunday afternoon teas, a weekly institution with the Porters.

I was first invited to a few of the Sunday afternoon gatherings, which were vaguely interesting, and where one occasionally met distinguished European or English visitors; but these parties were large and miscellaneous. It was my proudest social triumph that I was soon transferred from those Sunday gatherings to the list of dinner guests, a list much more select.

Mrs. Porter's dinners remain for me an archetype of the traditional formal style of entertaining, such as I knew from the novels of James. The seating of the guests was carefully planned: each man seated between two women, with each of whom in turn he conversed. The guests, whether one knew them in advance or not, might all be assumed to have their claims. Mrs. Porter aimed at a dinner party which included both gentlemen and ladies, especially the latter, whose claims were proper lineage and social position; stuffy, stiff little persons, but also, in equal measure, representatives of the intellectual world, Harvard professors, distinguished foreign visitors, and a few young men of some proven ability in the arts who offered promise of future distinction—the small group to which, by virtue of my *James* and my critical essays, I was taken to belong.

The food at Elmwood was delectable beyond any I had known. The cook was Italian, the wife of Angelo, who, in his white jacket, opened the door when one rang the bell at Elmwood. Angelo was Lucy Porter's prime specimen of her status, a butler who opened the door and served at dinner, while at Mrs. Warren's Mount Vernon Place house a womanservant in uniform of black dress and white apron opened, and two uniformed women waited at table, while poor Miss Nichols mostly had to open her own door and go out to a restaurant when she needed a real meal.

The food at Elmwood was delectable partly because it was European, and Italian, yet not the lower-class Neapolitan food I associated with Italian cookery, the kind I had had at American-Italian restaurants. The pasta was delicate and various. The sweet was likely to be some confection with chestnut paste as its foundation. I, who had never had such fare, could better have done justice to it had I been eating in a Benedictine refectory, the meal consumed while a lector read some well-written or at least edifying book, or, better still, have eaten alone and in silence. I have never mastered the art of eating and talking at the same time; so, if the talking is either stimulating, or socially obligatory, I forget to eat or at least to complete each course when my neighbors have completed theirs. At an Elmwood dinner, conversation was obligatory; I was therefore but dimly though delightedly conscious of what I ate.

I was content to talk, first to the lady on my right, and then the lady on my left. The whole art of social conversation engaged me. Not to be shy or gauche, not to be diffuse of words or specialized; to give and take; not to be too heavy or too light; too personal or too impersonal; not to be too brilliant or too witty: such are the desiderata.

After dinner, the men were left to their cognac and cigars or cigarettes, while the women withdrew to the drawing room. And then, twenty minutes or half an hour later, the men rejoined the women; and then one talked with those one had not sat with at dinner. The whole ritual at Elmwood was what I had read about in English novels but had never expected to share.

Mrs. Porter was neither beautiful nor elegant nor brilliant: nor in any other way stylized. It was her husband who had created the setting, the world, the ritual which she, proud of him and of his books and his international circle of friends—art historians and artists—felt it her obligation to continue. Her own attempts, made at dinner or other times, to draw out her international guests or dilate on their specialties, were unimpressive. Nor could she lead a conversation, as, in their ways, could Rose Nichols and even Mrs. Warren. But, with Elmwood around her, with the presence of Angelo the butler, and the aid of a social secretary, she managed to provide civilized evenings which meant very much to me, one of the youngest and (in status, though perhaps not in spirit) one of the humblest. I did not admire her; but I respected her and was grateful to her for keeping up a hospitable tradition.

Mrs. Kingsley Porter's husband, as art historian, had gone through many shifts of taste, but before his untimely death had become absorbed in the crosses and culture of Ireland, and, after a summer or two of renting, had bought a castle, Glenveagh, in Donegal, one of the northern counties of Ireland. After his death, Mrs. Porter continued to own the castle for some years; and in the summer of 1935, she invited me to spend a fortnight there.

I landed at Cobh, earlier Queenstown, and made my way in leisurely fashion to remote Donegal, stopping at Cork and Dublin, charmed by Ireland from the start. My fellow passengers, Boston Irish who landed at Cobh, asked me whether I had relatives there, and, when I said I had none, expressed amazement at my visiting Ireland, the most god-awful country they knew. They meant that there was no sanitation, or any other modern improvements, and that the land was poverty-stricken, and that trains didn't run on time, and that everything was dirty.

All that my fellow passengers implied of Ireland was true. Public places like bus stations were intolerably dirty; trains did not start on time, or buses either, and when a leisurely cow crossed the railroad track, the train courteously stopped up for the animal's transit. Going into a restaurant in Cork, late in the lunch hour, I looked for a clean tablecloth. The quick eye of the proprietress saw my search, and she spoke up reassuringly, "They'll not be replenished till the morrow."

Though I had not heard of them, except for St. Patrick's, I expected to find beautiful churches in pious Ireland. These were not to be found. The two cathedrals of Dublin, both in Anglican hands, St. Patrick's and Christ Church, are pre-Reformation, but never can have been beautiful, and now exist in Victorianly patched-up restorations, financed by the two leading brewery companies of Dublin. Beautiful ancient parish churches such as one sees everywhere in England in the smallest villages, are not to be found, either in Catholic or Anglican hands.

This appears not to be the result of the wars which have gone on in Ireland, but of Irish indolence and Irish imagination. The Irish are all extraordinarily gifted, whatever their degree of education, with eloquence, often of a Latinic sort. They are born visionaries and storytellers, and when I reflected on the almost total absence of architecture in Ireland, I was driven to the conclusion that poverty, indolence, and imagination were jointly responsible. With a wave of the hand and in the most beautiful English spoken anywhere in the world, a Dubliner could conjure up a word picture of the most beautiful cathedral you ever saw. As it was so much superior to anything one could actually build, why go to the bother of trying?

At Dublin I registered at the Shelburne, the best hotel, facing St. Stephen's Green, and with its menus printed in French. I should scarcely have registered in such a grand hotel had I not been given wise advice, by Miss Nichols, who explained that the cheapest room at the best hotel would be no higher than the best room at the poorest—which proved to be true. Near the Shelburne was the Irish senate, with guards pacing in front of it. As I lingered, wishing I could enter it, a tall and elegant gentleman approached me, and discovering my wish, introduced himself as an Irish senator. He not only took me for an inspection of the Dal in session, but invited me to tea thereafter. Learning that I was a literary man, he began, in a fashion unbelievable of a United States senator, to recite from memory early poems of Yeats, reciting them in his beautiful Dublin voice and accompanying them with waves of his fine, manicured hands.

Donegal, my ultimate destination, was a remote and ill-populated part of Ireland, with villages and manor houses separated by long distances. Though Mrs. Porter's castle was only nineteenth-century Gothic, it was built of granite and impressive. A long driveway led up to the castle, which fronted on a lake; and a terrace ran along the side of the dining room—a terrace on which lordly peacocks strutted and cried their piercing and melancholy cry. I was greeted at the entrance by a figure out of a Gothic novel: the butler, not the familiar Angelo but a man lean and cadaverous of face and hunched of figure, and dressed in somber black. He showed me to my room; and, doubling as a valet for poor gentlemen without any, unpacked my suitcase for me. Had I had evening clothes, he would have laid them out in time for my dressing for dinner. When I went to my room at night, the bed was open, that is, the bedclothes were folded back and my pajamas and slippers were laid out.

Life at Glenveagh was indeed idyllic. We breakfasted from the buffet, but at lunch and dinner were served by the butler. Every day we either entertained visiting county families, consisting of mother and two unmarried daughters, or the like, or were ourselves entertained. This at the noon meal. We drove long distances, the nearest county families living forty or fifty miles from us.

One day we had lunch at a seventeenth-century castle with husband and wife as our hosts. The wife showed us through the house, assuring me that she heard and saw ghosts every night, and indicating their whereabouts. I scrutinized her pale face closely and was convinced that she might be deluded, but was not inventing.

There were other guests at Glenveagh, too, for longer or shorter times—one of them Walter Starkie, professor from the University of Dublin, who had lived among the gypsies and written much about their music. We had an abundance of music and good talk. Yet what most remains in my mind of that enchanted fortnight is the beautiful Irish countryside and the elegant way of living of the civilized rich.

11

Becoming a Friend

My Boston is the city as it was between the two world wars, during and immediately after the depression: how far the city I invoke any longer exists I have no way of knowing. And I have to define myself in relation to Boston. A middle-class young man from Waltham, a working farmer's son from Stow, I am not of course a proper Bostonian—not of such families as are described in Cleveland Amory's book. I am, and was, in my Boston days, in the uncomfortable position of being neither a "Bostonian" from the right side of the Hill nor a rank outsider. In many ways, it might have been easier for me socially had I been an outsider—hence to be placed merely as a man of talent. To be a white Anglo-Saxon Protestant (ethnically a Protestant), yet not the member of a social register family, was an awkwardness, probably felt to be so by others, and by me even more.

The chief advantage of these defects was the anonymity it gave me. Had I been born in the class I partly envied, I would doubtless have had to be a rebel, like my friend Jack Wheelwright, who was born in it. I would have been no more at home with the "cold roast beef Boston" of the Apleys than I was in my own immediate family. Indeed, there is in me an ardor which makes me fit only for conscious adjustment to my fellow Yankees; Europeans, especially Italians and Greeks, are in many ways nearer to me than my compatriots. Were it not for my father's warmth and affection, I would indulge in the favorite fantasy of children alien to their family—that I was a love child or a foundling. The case is more complicated however; a reluctant Yankee, I still have the New England conscience along with an ill-consorting temperament.

Unlike the proper Bostonian, I inherited no world of relationships, no fixed circle in which I could, but also must, move. But it gave me great pleasure to entertain in my apartment, at tea and at cocktails. I excelled at the making of very dry martinis, the flow of which, heightening the conversation, went on generally from five-thirty to eight, when I and my guest or guests sallied out to one of the Hill's many good neighborhood restaurants.

Since I had a spare bedroom on my second floor, I could put up a friend for a night or a series of nights; one summer, my British painter friend, Dick Carline, made my apartment his pied-à-terre, from which he paid visits elsewhere and to which he returned. My old Wesleyan fraternity brother and friend, half Greek, half Nova Scotian, Paul Vaka, often came from his mastership at Choate School to visit. For a year, Benny Bissell tried out his vocation at the Cowley Fathers' monastery across the Charles, and regularly spent his weekly holiday with me. Another close friend and frequent caller was my distant cousin, Edward Flint, a Harvard graduate who had majored in philosophy and had studied the organ with Nadja Boulanger and had been a devoted and valued participant at St. Peter's School.

Then there were a few intellectually active and engaging members of the Boston University faculties, my approximate contemporaries, who were for longer or shorter members of my "circle": I think particularly of Charles Ramsay, a Tennesseean and an economist who took the philosophical rather than the statistical view of his subject, a man whom Benny and I had deemed indeed worthy of teaching his subject one summer at "the School."

Of another sort was Bjarne Bremer, a Scandinavian, who worked as masseur at the Sidney-Hill Health Club, of which for two years I was an alien but fascinated member; we met at our boundaries, he longing to be a literary man or an intellectual, and I longing in my Tonio Kroeger fashion, for the simple life of the well-disciplined body and a moderate prowess at handball, that gentlemanly form of exercise at which my inability to judge distance and to catch a ball rendered me a dub.

Friends brought acquaintances; and I remember, peripherally but warmly, Peter Pezzati, American-born Italian painter and Dante amateur, who, all one summer while he painted my portrait, vivified the sittings by quoting Dante or by intense, breathless discourse on aesthetics, and Arthur Johnson of Ipswich, a swarthy, lean, Byzantine-looking bachelor, who, a pure Yankee and reared a Methodist, had become (after an Anglican interlude) an ordained deacon in the Greek Orthodox Church.

Proud but unwarranted anxiety kept me from personal relations with Harvard men above the status of graduate students—an apprehension which I sadly and deeply regret in the case of F. O. Matthiessen, who once entertained me at lunch in his Hill apartment and with whom I had—as I most realized after his death—very much in common, in character as well as literary interests. But this barrier, this neurotic fear of presumption or attempted ascent, did not operate in the case of those at once academics and persons of intellectuality and integrity who were not Harvard professors. After the exchange of letters, I entertained Lester Bradner, of Brown, like myself a neo-Latinist, and Newton Arvin, of Smith, whose generous praise of my Hawthorne edition was praise indeed. Arvin I knew in the middle 1930s when he was at the height of his Marxist Communism and I at the center of my Chester-Belloc agrarian distributism: we met on the double ground of literary taste and personal integrity. But more characteristic were the alliances formed at this period with Helen White, a suburban Boston Irish Catholic, and a student of the interrelations of religion and literature, especially in the seventeenth century, who, teaching at the University of Wisconsin, came back to Boston for her vacations, and with William S. Knickerbocker, the then editor of the *Sewanee Review*, who, traveling between Tennessee and Maine, where he summered, never failed to stop for a visit with me, a contributor to his *Review*.

Some of these literary-academic folk I met at the annual conventions of the Modern Language Association, which I often attended, paying special attention to the meetings of the group called Poetics and General Aesthetics, the group which attracted Craig La Driere, W. K. Wimsatt, Ruth Wallerstein, and others concerned with literary theory; and these I kept in touch with also through intermittent correspondence. I was already an addicted letter writer, finding much of my intellectual stimulation, and indeed even reason for being, in what came and went by mail.

Then there were older people who climbed the two flights of stairs to my apartment, most notably my old friend the Reverend Louis Field Hite, the philosopher of the Swedenborgian Theological School and for three summers St. Peter's resident philosopher, dressed always in old-fashioned clerical garb, his black coat fitting too tightly around his neck to show more than a glimpse of his white collar—ever ready for resumption of discourse as abstract as I could manage. And Mrs. Irving Babbitt came, the perceptive, intuitive, cultivated widow of my old master, whose books and papers I had the honored pleasure of ordering after his death; and sometimes Mrs. Ernest Marriett, the widow of an Episcopal priest, herself a minor poet in the stricter forms, and the mother of a Harvard poet, who died young; and, upon a few occasions, Miss Rose Nichols of Mount Vernon Street.

Mostly, however, my guests were of my own age—somewhere in the thirties, or younger, of whom many names and many varied images hover now, not to be particularized. They were chiefly young men of artistic aspirations—young musicians, composers, pianists, and singers; or they were students of painting or architecture or the dance; or they were poets. These young men had some gift, some talent, some ambition: not enough of any of these "somes," especially of energy, ambition, work, persistence—those virtues of character without which no talent is brought to fulfillment.

My oldest friend, Benny Bissell, several years my senior, and from my freshman year at Wesleyan, my chief teacher and guide, put up, during my early years of the thirties, a vigorous fight to maintain me in a state of docility and pupilage. Benny had no intention of having his approximate domination of me challenged by others, whether older or younger. He was jealous of my new acquaintances and determined that I should establish no rival friendship. By gossip, wit, satire, irony, and patronizing tone, he tried to expose the claims of any formidable newcomer and to hold his own sway. But, in so behaving, he surrendered so much of what I had valued him for—his intelligent and dignified suffering at the hands of barbarians—that he lost his battle and almost terminated our friendship.

Benny's strategy was to draw me back to our decade and a half of shared memory—of Wesleyan and "the School," to the past—to try to reduce me, in relation to him, to the dimensions of the naive but energetic and vaguely and crudely aspiring and ambitious undergraduate he had first known. Properly, I resented this reductionism. In my thirties, I felt too young thus to be constricted to memory. I felt perfectly competent to face the present, and the future, too, and to make a new start.

Two younger men came into my life during the first year after my return from London, where, through Eliot and Dick Carline and letters of introduction to connections of the James family, I had, with the immunities of a foreigner, experienced a much more varied and imaginatively exciting social world than ever before. I returned to Boston with an appetite for people and a confidence in my ability to make friends, that ability which, through early life, I had so conspicuously lacked.

Wallace Fowlie and Howard Blake, the former ten years my junior, the latter fifteen years, were both met—I delight to trace back how particular friendships have been made—through superior students of mine at the College of Practical Arts. Wallace's poet cousin Pauline, a shy, proud, palely beautiful girl, mentioned her cousin in an essay or conversation or both, probably as a poet and lover of music (the name Debussy was one signal I caught); and, in writing an essay on Poe, another young woman, the daughter of a state senator from Maine, described a young poet friend of hers whose dress and pallor and nocturnal habits resembled Poe's, were perhaps modeled on his. The requisite first meetings were arranged.

Both of these younger men were, like me, native Yankees, both from the middle class, both bookish, literary, musical, artistic: in a sense, younger Austins, but with the distinct advantage over me of being, so I soon felt, far more focused and clear of aim—not, as I was, on the boundary, torn between options and alternatives. Neither had more energy than I; neither perhaps had as much; but theirs they did not disperse or squander—these fortunate young artists, who were sure that they were literary men, writers even.

My habitual epitaph for myself is "Desiring this man's art and that man's scope." I envied these young men their assurance, their clear sense of vocation, their never doubting that they were writers. Was it their influence which made me, despite my waverings and self-doubts, settle upon *writer* as the name for my own vocation? In drawing away from Benny and being drawn toward these two young writers, my juniors, I was certainly, at the least, choosing the direction in which I willed to move, choosing my influence.

The matter of influence was not, of course, one-sided, for there were things I had to impart as well as to receive, even though I was ever far more conscious of what I received. There was something very New England about both those friendships: each teaching what he knew best to his friend; each friend grasping every opportunity to learn from his own private tutor. What real education I have received has come mostly through my friends.

Wallace was for me a unique combination of artist and pedagogue, the two existing side by side without seeming conflict. A
born ritualist as well as a symbolist, he had, in his apartment, a
black desk at which he corrected his students' exercises and a
white writing table at which to compose his novels and poems.

For public teaching as well as private, he had a passion; and I
occasionally heard him lecture—a treat, for his lessons (as, after
the French fashion he liked to call them) were elegant as well as
lucid, elegantly lucid, carefully planned, proportioned, timed, so
as, exactly, to end on the hour; often memorized; delivered with
eloquence and precision of enunciation. His model for these performances was his Harvard teacher, André Morize, a master of the
French *explication de texte*; and, even in his early twenties, Wallace—or Michel, as I now call him (for his private, his secret name,
which I always used, was French—Michel Wallace) was already a
minor master at the half-pedagogic, half-aesthetic mode of discourse.

Michel taught me how to make French onion soup. He also
sought to teach me to drive an automobile, though he gave up,
without a word, after the first lesson. He likely tried to teach me
handball, for it was through him, already a member, that I joined
the health club. He was better rounded and balanced than I, and
far more sensible and practical and systematic: here, New England
and his adopted France collaborated.

Even his writing was systematic, regular, habitual: so many
pages a day; so long at his desk, generally early in the morning.
From time to time, I tried to emulate his habits of regularity at the
writing table, generally unable to persist for long. My own writing,
of which I did much, was done chiefly by spurts and at irregular
hours. When I had an assignment, a commission, as I liked to have,
the deadline served me as a point at which to start sprinting, while
Michel had regularly ready his manuscript (neatly typed by himself) well in advance of any publisher's need.

Michel had just graduated from Harvard College when I first
met him, and was pursuing his graduate studies at Harvard and
doing part-time teaching at a private school. He took a doctorate
(philosophically exacting) at least as easily as I took my Princeton
degree, and apparently in much the same spirit. He had an excellent memory, a fine and early trained ear for language, and a docility, real or feigned. Under his academic coloring, his unbohemian,
almost businessman, certainly professional exterior, he remained

undistorted, almost unaffected, by the methods, routines, and aims of academic scholarship.

His prime ambition was to write—and to publish; and, to do both, he, no more than I, needed the conventional academic invitations. And, businessman as well as artist, already, when first I knew him, he knew how to separate the writer from the salesman. When he received manuscripts back, he immediately sent them out again and continued to circulate them till they were placed. If he could not find an American publisher, he found an English, or a French. Bilingual, he could and would, if necessary, translate his book just written from one language into another. This last was a practice I could not follow; but I was fortified, if not influenced, by Michel's assiduity in marketing his wares into a similar and equally successful persistence in the disposition of my own.

In one matter which concerns writing we differed. I was accustomed to having my productions criticized, and, with whatever wincing at some of the judgments offered, desired criticism; but Michel soon made it clear to me, and in so many words, that he wished no analysis or advice, even constructive. I desisted. But that was a part of a larger difference: he was it seemed almost entirely intuitive in his mental operations; I, something of a dialectician or arguer as well.

Between friends, there is likely to be some special form of sharedness, some mode of communication. Ours was an affectionate session of French, poetry and diction and criticism; such sessions went on for several years. Those were memorable more or less weekly afternoons. We read together Gide—Les nourritures terrestres, Baudelaire, Rimbaud, Mallarmé; we talked of Proust's asthma jacket, of which Michel had an equivalent to wear when he wrote. The pattern of these afternoons included reading the texts aloud. How Michel's sensitive ear could have endured my crude enunciation I cannot understand; but here, the pedagogue and the lover of all things French came to his aid: for, during the period of his tutelage, I made progress, if I read slowly, in rendering the French u and o and the nasals not too barbarously. The reading was accompanied by commentary—Michel contributing, as I recall, what he had learned from his Harvard professors and French scholarship, and I improvising explications and interpretive comments on my critical own; without all this being able to make my contribution, I could probably not have endured being an elementary pupil in French diction. Michel's French was, then, like that of the few other American-born French scholars I have known, mandarin: precise and elegant beyond that of those born French.

Michel and I had many tastes and interests in common, even a native religiosity of temperament and a movement toward Catholicism. I could see how he, though the most tender, respectful, and dutiful of sons, had been drawn out of the Baptist and Fundamentalistic religion in which he had been reared, and out of his suburban environment and class by the intensity of his devotion to two causes—France and poetry. It would be hard to say which of these came first, either chronologically or metaphysically, causally, psychologically. In a sense, poetry stood for France, and France for poetry, each being a transcendent incarnate.

Chronologically, French seems to have come first, for Brookline, the Boston suburb where Michel grew up, had early introduced the study of French into the grammar school: and he began his French in the sixth grade under charming and ardently Francophile lady teachers. French was his initiation into the exotic and Romantic; the first evocation of all which was not suburban. And everything connected with France had its magic: the words, the morphology, history, geography, cuisine, music. He could imagine it all before ever he paid his first visit to Paris; and, when I once asked him whether, on that first visit, he found what he expected, he replied, "Exactly." He received no surprise, only glad confirmation. I could see clearly how this early attachment to France had educated my friend—as other attachments to other civilizations, Italy or Greece, have educated other Americans. And I in turn had the prized advantage of seeing France, and reading French literature, through Michel's expert and addicted eyes.

Of the poets I thus read with Michel, it was Mallarmé who most reached and impressed me. Here I seemed to have found *poésie pure*, hermetical, magical, poetry written, poetry existing as an object unconnected with human feelings, something recondite and arcane. I was too moral and humanistic to devote my life to the exegesis of poetry so pure (as technical as philosophy); but Mallarmé's poetry—or the idea of it—made a deep and permanent impression on me as an ultimately conscious, carefully chosen and willed kind of life as well as composition.

If Michel was the priest of poetry, Howard Blake was the poet; and if *genius*, a Romantic term, is to stand unavoidably for an abstract and ideal archetype, I can say that Howard was the closest approximation to it I have ever intimately observed: not only the poet but the genius—the latter shown not only in his art and his passionate identification with that art but his whole highly intuitive nature, which sized up so quickly any situation and dictated to him how to handle it.

First meeting him, then a thin and pale youth of seventeen, carefully dressed in a dark blue suit with white shirt and black tie, and careful of his diction, I could see the superficial resemblance to Poe; and I had already heard of his living mostly by night. But only gradually did I take in the larger, the more basic, resemblance—and only later the larger dissimilarities between these "fallen aristocrats."

I was immediately drawn to Howard, and fascinated by him, but also baffled. His life story, though that of a fellow Yankee, had been so unlike my own, sounded so melodramatic, that I was doubtful whether to credit it: only slowly, after finding no significant variations in the story told me by installments, did I conclude it substantially true.

His parents, the Blakes and the Sanfords, came from southern New England; and his boyhood home was in Wollaston, a part of Quincy. Howard and his sister Eleanor were the children of a second marriage. The second Blake marriage broke up when the son was eight or ten. His mother (after having had other lovers) ran away with a married man; his father went insane and was confined. Howard was taken over by a wealthy uncle, who found a home for him in Lexington with a married insurance clerk. At Lexington, he went to school, was unhappy, tormented by other boys at school and by the clerk's family. He was then transferred to a private day school at Hartford for a year or two of junior high school. That ended his formal education. He came to Boston, presumably as the big city, "the metropolis of New England" (so Cotton Mather called it), lived at the YMCA for a time. His uncle found him a menial job or two, which he couldn't, for long, endure.

But he began to make friends among other artistic and semi-antibourgeois spirits, chiefly older men; one of them a Latin master at the Brookline Country Day School; another a product of St. Paul's School, Concord, who had nearly graduated from Harvard, a gentleman of leisure and oriental sojourns. There were also older women, one of them the widow of an Episcopal priest, herself a minor poet, whose acquaintance I later made. There were also a few young men, one of these, a Nebraskan farm boy who had come to Boston to make his way, his only heritage a copy of Emerson which his idealistic mother had given him in lieu of the Bible. During this period of a year or two, Howard was dependent on these friends, none well-to-do, for his precarious living: his modest room rent and his meals, which he had to earn by his gifts and attentions: he had, as he used to tell me, to "sing for his supper": not, certainly, a dignified thing to do; but, fallen young gentleman that he was, and artist to boot, he seems to have felt that he had no real alternative. He would rather have perished, it seems, than to have worked from nine to five at any occupation for which he could have qualified. And indeed he seemed physically unable to carry on everyday wage earning, whether physically or psychosomatically. He fainted easily when first I knew him, whether through near-starvation or through anxiety.

His pride did not allow him to reveal to me his precarious mode of living, and it required some open words addressed to me by one of his contemporaries, a young pianist and composer, for me to take in his situation, to which my New England mind, reared to regular education, regular work, saving, and planning, knew no New England analogue. "Did I know that Howard was starving?" No, I didn't. Of course I must help a young man at once so pitiful and so admirable, a destitute poet. I was a professor of English whose special field was poetry; I earned my livelihood teaching the works of the dead poets. Surely, I felt, I had the responsibility to provide for a living poet in need, such a real and promising poet as, after a few months of acquaintance, I judged him to be.

Gradually, step by step, I took over his support, a fact concealed from his friends, as well as from mine, by a convenient fiction. My benevolence was never easy, or wholly ungrudging, so contrary to all my rearing was Howard's way of life—which might be called support by a patron. Why couldn't he earn a living like other people, and write poetry in his spare time—as I wrote my critical essays or Michel wrote his? One answer was clear: he couldn't because he was not a university graduate. But why, then, not send him through Harvard? I did think of that, but he had not graduated from high school; and with his pride and his claims, his already semipublic status as a poet, it would be too humiliating for him to resume public school again.

In the course of time, we decided that a grand tour of Europe should be Howard's approximate equivalent of a college education; and in 1937 he left on such a self-charted journey through England, Germany, Austria, France, and Italy. He had nine months of liberty for all kinds of experience, and used them to the full. I thought him lavish of my money; but I reflected that he at least, as I did

not, knew how to use luxury without either guilt or the constitu-
tional New England failure to enjoy.

But there remained the problem of his immediate education:
he had no wish to utter a "barbaric yawp"—must be a scholar,
gentleman, literary poet. So his friends collaborated to educate him
by private tutoring. One taught him French, and another German;
another, an elderly gentleman, taught him all he knew—manners,
etiquette, oriental art, wines; and I was tutor-in-general. I too
taught all I knew: literature, music, theology—whatever I knew
which he wanted. No one undertook to teach him Latin, which I,
a Latin major, had naturally supposed indispensable to the writing
of elegant, literary English. To my amazement he learned not only
to use correctly difficult Latin words, but also elaborate sentence
structures—all from the care with which he read some of my favorite seventeenth- and eighteenth-century writers, notably Sir
Thomas Browne and Dr. Johnson (the *Lives of the Poets* and *Rasse-
las*).

He was a brilliant student. He applied himself to what he
wanted to know, knew he needed to know, had been convinced
by me that he ought to know, with a concentration and a sense of
direction and energy which astonished and impressed me. While
my Boston University students read excerpts from masterpieces,
he read whole books; and he remembered and could use what he
read. In his own poetry or in conversation, he could deploy effec-
tively all he knew.

I sometimes wondered whether I really knew or cared anything about poetry till I began to know Howard. To be sure, I had
already "loved" poetry vaguely, had written undergraduate poems,
had already been attracted to the metaphysical poets, had already
in London, bought the new poetry and attended poetry readings.
But I had no trained concern with aesthetic form and structure and
style. No teacher had given it to me, and I had not known how to
acquire it on my own. Poetry for me was still a kind of interest
derivative from my interest in religion and my interest in music.

Howard was not only (or even primarily) a reader of poetry;
he was himself a practicing poet. When I met him, he was also
already very style conscious and technique conscious: was writing
in the French forms—villanelles and the like and, copiously, in
sonnets. Now I knew a living poet—I who knew only readers,
students, and scholars of poetry, and who thought of poets as dead
or otherwise personally inaccessible. Now I had a chance to learn
what were the psychological sources and compulsions which made

poets poets—and also how particular poems were made. An example of the latter: sometimes, when we were in conversation, Howard would dart into my adjoining small study and rapidly write down a poem and hand it to me. I would eagerly reach for the product, suppose that it would be the product of something immediate—in our conversation or his situation. But it never was. Something had just released the poem, but the poem itself was something long incubated: his best poems were long brooded and often self-repetitive, like those of Poe or many other poets.

In early years of our friendship, we read or analyzed some contemporary poets and poems—chiefly the early Wallace Stevens and Hart Crane, but probably Eliot and also some Hopkins. We also worked together over Howard's own poems—their text, their verbal surface. The most characteristic and amusing sample I can manufacture is my friend's question, "Austin, what is a five-letter word, beginning with *F* and meaning 'innocence,' or: a word in two syllables meaning 'fear' and beginning with an *M*?" Under the instigation of such shared interests, I also wrote some poems. Howard revised, enriched, and much bettered these, poems thinner and more lucid than his.

At the end of the preface to my edition of Hawthorne, published in April 1934, I acknowledge the help of "my secretary, Mr. Howard Blake." This preface must have been written at the end of the summer of 1933, a summer which I entirely devoted to the job of editing, and especially to writing the long introductory essay— really a little book. This was, I recall, an uncommonly happy summer. Though it was hot, I worked away, with pleasure amounting to joy, in my Beacon Hill apartment; and Howard worked more closely with me on that than on any other of my literary enterprises.

In the preface to my *Crashaw* (1939), I "avow a large debt to the sensibility and critical wits" of Howard Blake, but he now is characterized as "friend."This book, so long in the making—something like ten years—would in all probability never have appeared as a book at all and certainly not as the kind of book it is had it not been for Howard. When he first met me, I was chiefly working on highly specialized and technical scholarly articles on Crashaw, the results of my London researches. My original intention of writing a critical book had been virtually abandoned, while I continued with minute scholarly investigations which might have gone on indefinitely. It was Howard who spurred me on to resume my book, and to make it something written with structure and style.

This specific help with my books was only part of his literary help. He encouraged my daring to write not only about dead authors but also about contemporary writers (Kenneth Burke, for one). His influence on my criticism was double. On the one hand he urged me to include stylistic analysis in all my essays. On the other hand he encouraged me to hold on to the sound part of my Babbittian inheritance—the philosophical part of me, which views literature as Weltanschauung. In literature, each of us could help the other, both theoretically and practically. Each in turn taught— and was taught. This, to my experience, and to my knowledge of literary history, is by no means an uncommon experience; it is almost a rule in the case of friendship between literary men, whatever their disparity in age.

But now I come to speak of ways in which Howard was distinctly and unreciprocally the teacher. He had a far clearer view of me as a man, a self, than I, unhappily vague and ill-defined of ego, had ever had. I had, in my youth, alternated between grandiose ideas of myself and other ideas utterly deflating and defeating. Howard, keenly intuitive, saw me both as I was, as I (so unsteadily) saw myself, and saw what, with love and some guidance, I was capable of becoming; he discovered the Platonic essence of Austin and was adept at devising means of making it an existence.

In my youth I had thought of myself as an artist and a genius: I had to think of myself in these ways—as superior to normal people for, if I wasn't, I was so palpably their inferior. My deviations from normal behavior I therefore took as stigmata accompanying my gifts. But these eccentricities were handicaps: they made it difficult for even well-disposed normal people to see how much real character and New England solidity, as well as real intellect, I had.

I had—and have had for life—the handicap of being unable to learn by imitating, the way normal people learn to walk, to dress, to open a can. I can't make that act of transfer. I can't take in, by observing, how other people do things. Howard soon saw this strange defect; and he loved me enough, and enough wanted to be proud of him he loved, to bother to teach me as I had to be taught: step by step.

Some steps forward I had made. At twenty-one, finding myself perforce a teacher in charge of students, my New England conscience came to my aid. I had a responsibility to perform, not only to culture but to young persons, not much younger than I: a responsibility to take a personal interest in my "parishioners" and "patients": I was a man "set under authority."

But personal relations with one's students should never become intimate—any more than a priest's with his parishioners. I
stood centrally in need of some more or less permanent love; yet
I was not ready for marriage: indeed it is fortunate that I did not
at that time attempt it. I needed a family of my own choosing, yet
a family not involving domesticity, for which I had then no wish.

During the 1930s, Howard was the central figure in my personal life. Our relationship was complex, rich, both constantly
shifting and underlyingly steady. He and I were both weak in some
ways and strong in others. During our years together in Boston,
these strengths and weaknesses were mutually complementary.

His central strengths, which imparted strength and courage to
me, were his integrity and his vitality. How many of my friends,
whether clerical or academic, seemed prim, cautious, negative,
prudent: feared life and commitment and adventure, including the
giving of themselves to others. Howard was on the side of affirma-
tion, of action, of boldness, of risk taking—in short, on the side of
life.

12

Becoming a Writer

In my youth I was fond of texts, biblical and humanist, of pensées, sententiae, aphorisms, sage sayings. I treasured, and quoted, Goethe's "Der Meister zeigt sich erst in der Beschraenkung" (the master shows himself above all in restriction, in self-limitation) and Carlyle's "Let a man find his work, and ask no other blessings," and wise words from Emerson, that master of the problem of vocation.

I thought that I understood them: but to apply them was another matter. My problem of the 1930s, with many interests and some aptitudes, was to define my vocation, which was only to be done by many givings up or (to use a more melodramatic word which corresponded to my feelings) renunciations—such renunciations as even the most modest achievement requires. One must, it seems, give up almost everything to be, or to do, anything.

In 1931, when I returned to Boston and to Boston University after my year's fellowship in London, I returned to a profession, that of English teacher, or, as I preferred to think of myself, teacher of literature. *Profession* and *vocation* are words between which I distinguished. By the former, I mean the publicly identifiable occupation by which a man earns his livelihood, performs his social function, while by the latter I mean something at once narrower and richer, something more private and spiritual. A man's vocation may be found as the center and life-giving source behind his professional work, related to it but not the same (as is the case with a literary critic who is also a professor), or unrelated except by coexistence (as Thoreau's writing was to his surveying).

Had I lived in any period before the nineteenth century, when already culture was drawing away from faith, I would undoubtedly have adopted the Church as my profession, free then to find my vocation as a mystic, a musician, a scholar, or a writer. In my own time, I shrank from committing myself early to a creed to which I felt I must thereafter subscribe through the rest of my life, or abandon my profession. Confronted with practical alternatives, I found teaching English the way of supporting myself which involved the least intellectual constriction. The English teacher has not even to accept a standard or traditional conception of what literature is, or what it does for its readers—still less, to espouse some particular view of life. He is partly an authority on a body of written and printed matter; he is partly also a public speaker and an oral interpreter of literary documents; he is partly a middleman or mediator between books and neophyte readers, an initiator of the young into the written treasures of their culture. In many ways, being an English teacher today is the equivalent of being a priest in earlier centuries: it is a relatively unspecialized profession requiring chiefly goodwill, literacy, and some general intelligence.

The teaching of English was, for me, an entirely honest way of earning a livelihood, the most congenial I could have found; I also believed it to have a limited social usefulness, even at Boston University's College of Practical Arts and Letters, the secretarial school at which I functioned. At this institution, I was a living representative of what had traditionally been meant by culture: I was also an apologist for the creative arts and for speculative thought. My professional hours were long; but what I did outside of them was a matter of my discretion. That I publish was so far from being emphasized by the dean of the college that it might indeed rather have been used to show that I was neglecting my teaching, had there been any evidence for such a view. All which was required of me was to be locally useful—a diligent reader of student essays and blue books, a director of dramatics or debate or (as in my case) the glee club, a friendly adviser of the young women committed to my care.

Teaching at the college took time and energy, yet it gave me no sense of deep inner satisfaction. After a few years of it, I could discharge my professional duties with relative ease. I understood what older professors meant when they spoke of teaching and, then, of finding time for their "own work," by which they commonly meant research, the compilation of obscure facts for some scholarly article, by publication to be submitted to the judgment of their peers; and I saw the spiritual necessity of having some such work of my own. I had need of a vocation in addition to my profession: of something which I could do from center, which should engage the whole of me.

To find this was a matter negative as well as positive. Unavoidably, the roads not taken as well as the road selected both must appear, in summary, to involve more deliberate, conscious, and unwavering choice than was, or perhaps, could be, the case. Negatively I had to renounce some three potential vocations which had hovered over me in the 1920s.

In the 1920s, I had been cofounder of St. Peter's, a summer school of utopian sort, what would now be called a free university. This brief summer importance and authority considerably sustained me during the years of being a nearly anonymous and powerless graduate student or college instructor. The school was indeed my equivalent for the little magazine, the privately financed periodical of poetry such as some of my literary contemporaries were briefly operating as vehicles for their egos and their creeds. For ten years it fulfilled my sense of vocation: was that in which all my talents and interests converged. But after I returned from my perspective-giving year in London, it was evident that this delightful but also exhausting enterprise in community must be renounced.

Another activity I must renounce was church music, at which, in the 1920s, I had liked to think of myself as semiprofessional. Indeed, all through my teens and twenties, I felt myself—accurately, so far as I can judge—to be nearer to mastery at the keyboard than at the writing table. My hands, so inept at practical manual operations of the simplest sort, did, at the organ, obey my will. Church music made a deep appeal to me as uniting two of my concerns and devotions, religion and art; and it was thus, like the school, a form of vocation for me. But too, it was exhausting as well as exhilarating. As my mind developed, music, my first form of expression, had to take a subordinate place.

A musical amateur I did remain. I owned a succession of reed organs, and for a few years a Dolmetsch clavichord. My interest was centered on contrapuntal music of the seventeenth and eighteenth centuries. By Babbitt, I had been converted from sheer Romanticism to what was at first a merely doctrinal classicism, in music as well as literature. In my thirties, I was already "civilized" enough to prefer, to my old Romantic extemporizations, the ordered discipline of counterpoint—to find an even more satisfactory release by letting precise musical patterns give shape to my emotions. But all this was now my private discipline—that of a man who plays for his own pleasure—for self-expression in another medium than language, and for the education of his own sensibility.

Something else I had to subordinate to amateur status was philosophy, abstract thought, a concern for which, and a limited but genuine capacity for which, developed in me ten years later than my talent at music. As I began to show signs of having a mind, two friends of my youth, much older than I, both professional philosophers, Professors Edgar S. Brightman and Lewis Hite, took me in hand and gave me their private tutelage, which continued throughout my thirties. Neither thought to make a technical philosopher of me; both credited me with not being content to do what one of them, in a phrase which remains to sting and spur me, called "loose, literary thinking," that is, fuzzy pseudothinking, the rhetorical stringing together of relatively abstract terms. And both they, and Robert Luce, a young philosopher, a Harvard graduate student, introduced me to the names and the books of the great philosophers of the West.

According to Coleridge's familiar dictum, all men are born either Platonists or Aristotelians (the latter term covering, I take it, all kinds of empiricists). I was clearly a Platonist, an idealist; and the classic systems to which I was drawn were those of Plato, Plotinus, and Hegel; with special pleasure I read the British neo-Hegelians, Bosanquet and F. H. Bradley. But the reading of philosophy which I did in my twenties and thirties gave me the discipline of following a closely reasoned argument—no matter from what premises and no matter to what conclusions. I read, on my own, Locke, Hume, William James, and Santayana, as well as Platonists and Hegelians, profiting not only by the logic but by the philosopher's precision of language.

Philosophy *as such*, however, was too abstracted from human affairs, from the passions and the emotions, for it to have become my vocation. I preferred to study philosophy through its history, and to study *that* as reflected in the history of theology. I was particularly drawn to the history of dogma during the first six Christian centuries. Theology, though relatively abstract, is tied to a pair of concretions—on the one hand, religious experience and on the other, the sacred texts which record religious experience and the apostolic reflections upon those experiences. Biblical exegesis also interested me. Hermeneutics, the science of interpretation of texts, which plays so important a part in the New Critical study of literature, owes much to its fount. Systematic theology,

philosophy of religion, comparative religion, mysticism, and ecclesiastical history were even more central. During my twenties, I did
the reviewing of books on these subjects, both for the *New-Church
Review* and the *Living Church*, the Anglo-Catholic weekly; and I
published some essays on theological and ecclesiastical matters.
In those years I was, whether I used the phrase or not, a "lay
theologian"—a role more suited to my meditative mind than ever
any official priesthood could have been.

Music and theology were, more than literature, my characteristic interests in the 1920s. And they remained, throughout my
thirties and much longer, the poles of my spiritual world: sometimes I was nearer the sensuous and concrete pole; sometimes
nearer the abstract, conceptual, and systematic. Yet literature, always present, now grew relatively stronger as my center.

To give up the hovering thoughts of other possible vocations
was painful; but I tried to put the situation positively. I was not
called upon to surrender these old interests but to subordinate and
reconcile them in a true and unique vocation to which I was called
by the totality of my interests, tastes, aptitudes, and aspirations.
This vocation must for me be some kind of writing. I had begun
in 1922 to keep journals of the sort represented for me by those of
my spiritual ancestors, Emerson and Hawthorne—and by those of
the more distant kinsmen, Amiel and Chekhov. Journal writing
has continued all my life what it actively began to be in the 1930s,
my surest way of finding who I am and what I am about and what
I really think.

Writing, first, in my journals, and then in essays, was the best
method I knew for finding my way, with a minimum of pressures
and appeals from without, from the classroom of students or an
arguing company of friends—to what I really believed—not only
about literature, my professional discipline, but about "first and
last things," about principles—political, social, ethical, and religious. There were all my own inner voices to adjust to each other,
to arrange according to their priorities. I saw that my own salvation lay in writing—that is, in an honest facing and ordering of
my inner voices—those of the liberal democrat, of the spiritual
anarchist, and of the hierarchic authoritarian. Some kind of partial
oxymoron was needed to express my stance: an aristocratic noun
or verb, qualified, but not wholly negated, by its accompanying
democratizing adjective or adverb. My desire to write—that is, to
give some precise articulation to my thoughts and feelings, to put
on paper what I made of my experiences —was primary. But writ-

ing was indeed something more basic: my best mode of finding—I had often the sense of creating—a self.

Like Proust and Henry James, two of my greatest mentors, I, too, found no crude and brute experience of life satisfactory in itself; it was the meditation upon it, the interpretative ordering of it, which finally mattered. After a social evening, in encounter with many intense and vivid persons, it was the following hour of analyzing the course of the evening in intimate talk with one other which was the richest part. That other, in the absence of a collaborating other, I could myself supply, indeed, I must utter the final word.

What medium my writing was to take was a matter for exploration. In my Wesleyan days I wrote poems—bad imitations of Romantic poets. In my thirties, I tried again, under auspices which I think more suitable for me, as well as more recent, for I was now reading Crane and Ransom, Donne and Hopkins: I completed, and published, four poems which still seem to be professional, if minor. But, having demonstrated that I could, I felt no ambition to write further poems. I valued the discipline of writing in strict forms: I hold that everyone should, without pretensions or self-consciousness, write poems or sets of verses, and especially, every literary man should: my unliterary grandfathers and my great-grandmother did so; so do younger academic friends of mine. However, the dogmas of my generation, in which I shared, proclaimed the metaphor was central to poetry; and I found myself unsupplied with fresh metaphors. The style of which I was capable was to secure its effects through rhythm and syntax, through diction and the arrangement of sentence elements, not through immediate vision; it was to be the style of a meticulous prose.

At least three close friends who knew me in my early decades urged me to write novels. They thought me too "creative" to be either a scholar or a critic. My talk suggested that I could write dialogue. My sympathy and my empathy, my gift of drawing people out, my talent for controlling a social occasion, all seemed to suggest the writing of fiction. Yet I have among my manuscripts no unfinished novel. The qualities in me which suggested a novelist were certainly present, but they had to be aroused, it appears, by an actual situation, by physical presences. Then too, like most New Englanders, past or present, I took very little interest in story, in narrative as such; yet I was not modern enough to suppose that the novelist could dispense with story.

I am not, I am sure, a frustrate poet or novelist; I am not a critic by default. I am some kind of combination of artist (by temperament and concerns) and conceptualist. My prime interest is in understanding the literary work of art to the fullest possible degree, through all the means and techniques by which that understanding may be gained; and then I am interested in studying the role which art, especially the literary art, plays in life, and in the relations of that art, both in general and in particular, to the other chief disciplines and modes of interpretation, philosophy and religion. I am interested in the creative process—what makes people write, their habits of work (and that imaginative play of mind which goes before and into the work); I am interested also in the outcome of the work of art as it reaches and affects its readers. I am, in short, interested in both practical criticism—the analysis *and* evaluation of specific works of art—and in literary theory, the generalizations and assumptions which precede and follow specific judgments.

I find it easy to slip into the view that novels exist in order that they may receive expert treatment; that poems exist in order that they may be interpreted and fitted into some systematic theory of poetry. If *fin de siècle* poets could feel that the final end of the world is that it may all be taken up and consummated in a poem, I may be tempted to the view that the poem, in turn, is to be consummated by its absorption into a critical essay. But these are professional temptations to glorify one's own kind of making beyond all others. Common sense can be trusted to supply their counteractants.

There was one more choice I had to make, that between scholarly writing and criticism. This was the really hard one.

One reared as I was in a graduate school has drilled into him, by almost all of his teachers, that the aim of professional literary study is not the enjoyment of literature but its historical understanding. The former is for the undergraduate or the layman; it is more or less dismissed by the scholar as mere private opinion, impressionism, a matter of taste, not susceptible of scientific (i.e., objective) treatment—a matter for the journalistic critic on the one hand and the great critics on the other. The aim of the latter is not the acquisition of broad, general, massive, encyclopedic erudition, that grandiose aim which began to disappear after the seventeenth century. The proper aim of scholarship, my teachers held, or professed to hold, is the advancement of learning by the discovery of new facts, however trivial—by "research."

This scholarly keyword or slogan almost defies definition, so pervasive and loose is its engagement. It is a kind of academic busywork; it is detective work; it is the creation of single bricks for a hypothetical building which neither the brickmaker himself nor any one else may ever have occasion to use. It is reading some books, preferably rare, in a library which one has to cross the ocean or at least a continent to visit. All of these are descriptions by hostile satirists. Yet I know both the pleasure of research (the following of some minute line of inquiry, the solving of some biographical puzzle) as well as its frequent necessity. And the appropriate kind of research is practiced by the literary critic, though he commonly conceals it, calls it his "homework": it is the preparatory reading around his subject and his intellectual exercises, of which he publishes only the outcome, the conclusions at which he has arrived.

The Princeton Graduate School practiced, at least in my time, a toned down and urbane version of scholarship as research—a less rigorous version than that of Harvard. Furthermore, I had been already indoctrinated by Irving Babbitt, who, orally and in his book *Literature and the American College*, inveighed against the German system with its emphasis on the Ph.D. I passed my two years at Princeton firm in my humanistic principles, and, with a minimum of compromise, if any, took my doctorate. The real impact of historical scholarship reached me only belatedly, when Ronald Crane, the one scholar in the field whom I respected, published a review of my doctoral dissertation *Pope as Critic* (1929)—who, while generously praising it, found in it evidences of superficial, unscholarly preparation (words he did not use). In 1931, I was still vague and unsteady in my ideal for myself; I was more disturbed by the censure than heartened by the praise. So I read Crane's articles; studied *Modern Philology*, the scholarly quarterly he was then editing; and tried my hand at every type of technical research, pursuing every kind of byroad in studies of Crashaw and Pope. Between 1930 and 1933, I published a series of exact transcriptions of manuscripts in the British Museum and other libraries, and learned how to read the seventeenth-century handwriting of the Buttery Books at Peterhouse College, and calculated on what days Easter fell during the years Crashaw was writing his weekly poems for *Epigrammata Sacra*. Some of these activities had minor results for my eventual book on Crashaw, published in 1939; but, at the time, my chief motive was to demonstrate to myself and to others (including Crane) that I knew what scholarship was and was becoming an exact scholar as rapidly as I could. The graduate school system had, then, even though by delayed reaction, its strong effect upon me—a lasting one, and one partly beneficial, since it, together with my early training at the hands of the philosophers, gave me an increasing desire for exactness and precision—with facts (if with them I was dealing) or with ideas, or with words.

About 1934, I thought to myself that in order to become a reputable critic, I must first make of myself an "exact" scholar, so that no one could charge that I took up criticism to escape from the rigors of scholarship. But, to my naive surprise, when I first started to write criticism, I found that one mastery did not unconsciously train one for the next: though I had made myself a scholar, I still had to learn now to become a critic. I had to start all over again on a new career, with a new ambition.

For a much longer time, I tried, to myself and in writing, to define and defend the idea of the scholar-critic—one who unites in his own person two often separated and sometimes mutually hostile activities. In the 1930s, before the poets and novelists and critics migrated to the university to earn a secured livelihood and to teach creative writing and contemporary literature, the academic, the professor, was (or was supposed to be) a historical scholar; his opposite was the journalistic critic, in the tradition of Poe and Huneker, who reviewed current books, who was the proponent of the literary present, as the professor was of the literary past. Stuart Sherman, one of Babbitt's former students, though a Ph.D., was—and this in the mid-1920s—the first man to pass from the academy to journalism, and not the happiest example of the attempt of one bold man to unite the functions of both. But I believed the reconciliation still to be possible.

If Ronald Crane took my *Pope* seriously enough to give it careful review, I was equally affected by the serious tone in which John Ransom, poet-critic high in my esteem, publicly criticized my "Scholar and Critic: An Essay in Meditation" (1936). In his "Criticism, Inc.," reprinted in *The World's Body*, 1938, he indeed proved to me that it was not an effective program for the literary reform of English departments—if I had intended it as such a program. I imagine I had not; had merely attempted an apologia, or personal solution. But, unlike Crane's criticism, Ransom's fortified me.

The 1930s was the decade during which I turned from being a scholar to being a critic. I did not—and could not, because of my graduate school training or my New England heritage or both, renounce my habits of working up a subject as a scholar; but I did change my methods and my goal, which goal became the interpretation and evaluation of literary texts.

My method of composition correspondingly changed. I had been taught at Princeton to copy out extracts from books onto 3 × 5 cards. Thus, in writing my *Pope*, I had assembled my cards on the desk, arranged them and then transcribed them—composing transitions between the quotations. My part of the book was literary Scotch tape; my total book was a mosaic to which I had supplied the cement. Now, by way of reaction, I reverted to older, less "professional"methods of work. When I prepared to write a critical essay, I copied my quotations into notebooks, and constantly reread my notebooks as well as the annotations I had penciled in the margins of my heavily underlined texts. And the structure of an essay was now my own work, not dictated by the assembled quotations—of which now, indeed, I used but a sparse selection, "wasting" much material preparatorily accumulated.

I published my three books within a decade—*The Elder Henry James*, primarily an intellectual biography, based on some five years of research; and an edition of Hawthorne's *Sketches and Tales*, with a long introductory essay, which brought me some temporary reputation as a Hawthorne scholar-critic; and, lastly, *Crashaw*. Of these, the first two still show me adhering far too closely to my graduate school training; I string together quotations, chiefly long ones. In writing the *James*, I became so impregnated with the Jamesian ether that my transitions read like a toned down version of James's own style: were the quotation marks to be removed (after the fashion of the later Van Wyck Brooks) I doubt whether one who heard it read aloud could tell where James leaves off and Warren begins.

The *Crashaw*, completed at the end of the decade, is the first of my books which I can still read without too much wincing. It is overwritten, especially the lush last paragraphs of the conclusion, which it took a summer to write; but I did, in the very process of composing that book, pass from scholarship to criticism—without which passage the book, I am quite sure, would never have become a book, but would have remained an assemblage of specialized articles, most of them representing research in its narrowest sense. Only the steady help of a few friends, at once close and literary, held me to the making of a real book. One of them in particular, the poet, had the faith in me which I had not then in myself—that I could use as a critic the significances to emerge from the facts which I had accumulated as a scholar, and that I could write these significances up as a literary man.

By 1939, I had published three books in the three different worlds of English neoclassicism, of nineteenth-century American literature, and of English metaphysical poetry. So, I had already, without at the time conscious of it, decided against being that purest of scholars, one who specializes, who limits himself to the study of a single author ("a life for a life," as I used to put it) or a single period. And in this decision I had moved in the direction of criticism.

During this decade, I found that the book was less the form, or the length, for me than the essay. In considerable contrast to my oral style, my desire in writing was for compactness. My characteristic revision was to excise. I wanted my critical essays to be the equivalent of a book—its concluding chapter, so to speak. Willing to do the work for a book, after doing it, I wanted to offer only its essence, its "fundamental brainwork"—reducing what might have been chapters to paragraphs, and seeking to make each sentence what used to be called a topic sentence. In this ever increasing desire for compression, I was strongly influenced by the essays of writers so seemingly disparate as Emerson and Eliot. Like both, I thought to cut off all mere "gracious twaddle," in the Jamesian phrase, and to make my essay consist entirely of close, solid perception, without formal preface and, still more, without formal conclusion—that final paragraph of summary calculated to dispense the reader from reading the whole.

This drive for compactness, however, this desire to compress everything into a single sentence, to say all at once, was opposed by another desire—that of writing essays readable in themselves— not only about literature but themselves literature. On the whole, it is the second desire which prevailed in the 1930s: my essays on George Herbert and E. M. Forster are both readable and humanistic.

Two signs stand out as the signs of my passage from scholarship to criticism. In the 1930s, I took some contemporary subjects—not only Forster, on whom I wrote one of the earliest studies, but Kenneth Burke, who had then published only *White Oxen,* his book of short stories, his novel of declamations, *Towards a Better Life,* and his first book of criticism, *Counter-Statement.* Burke I chose, partly for the generic variety of his works, partly for his congeniality, but partly because he was not yet established and published on. I worked him up, as I had been in the habit of doing with dead and canonized authors. My hundred-page typescript, published in two installments of a critical quarterly, followed the traditional pattern of "the man and his work." But there was a significant difference. To Burke, living, indeed only two years my senior, I could address letters and engage in correspondence. My biographical sketch was based on what he had supplied.

The other sign was my appearance in two critical magazines, the *Sewanee Review*, then edited by William S. Knickerbocker, to whose early encouragement I owe much, and the *American Review*, edited (and financially maintained) for the four years of its existence by a wealthy young man, Seward Collins. In those days the *Sewanee* did not pay its contributors, chiefly rising young scholar-critics in the unversities; but Collins did; and I had the feeling of having become a real professional when, instead of reprints in payment, I received substantial checks.

In the case of both magazines, I began doing reviewing; in both cases, I graduated to having my essays accepted—not essay-reviews but independent productions. I much prefer to differentiate the two genres, despite illustrious contrary practice; for it seems to me that a new book should be closely and carefully reviewed as *such*, not made merely the pretext for an abstract of the book the reviewer would have written had he undertaken to write such a book. Meanwhile, a proper review requires almost as much work as an independent essay; yet can scarcely, in any sense, count for as much.

My participation in the *American Review* was variously a rich experience of a kind which I have not been able to duplicate. Collins ran a magazine, without advertisements, which paid its contributors, which had a bold and coherent editorial policy. His aim was to operate a *conservative* review which should juxtapose on its pages four existing right-wing groups—the New Humanists (the party of Babbitt and More, with T. S. Eliot as an ally); the British distributists (Belloc, Chesterton, and Arthur Penty); the French neoscholastics (Gilson and Maritain); and the southern agrarians and regionalists (Ransom, Tate, Davidson, and Robert Penn Warren). Though I had started from the New Humanism, I found the other groups also congenial. It was in the pages of the *Review* that I first met with the distributists and the regional agrarians; and I assimilated their doctrines, becoming a New England regional humanist, Catholic-minded. I read every number of the *Review* from cover to cover; I "learned while I earned." From this participation I derived an important, general cultural education, especially in social thinking, in which I had hitherto taken little interest.

Almost equally important—more so in some respects—for me as a writer was the fact that, once I had established myself with Collins and Geoffrey Stone, his assistant, as a reliable contributor (as indeed, among the collaborating groups the nearest to a synoptic figure, even though as yet unknown as a critic), the *Review* accepted everything I judged suitable and worthy to send in. It was a warming, heartening, confidence-giving, sustaining experience: this of being regularly assured of publication, and in a review with the general character of which I felt in general accord.

So, in the 1930s, I passed from being a scholar to being a critic. Perhaps I have never quite shed the hyphenation and become a critic pure and simple. But I have aimed at transcending by including the scholarship necessary as base for any sound criticism, and have found the very endeavor salutary. Criticism is first of all interpretation, but it must finally complete itself in evaluation, either implicit, like the very selection of an author on whom to write, or a topic—or explicit, an estimate on principles aesthetic or other, clearly stated—an act of comprehensive judgment which is the act of a responsible self.

This act of judgment does not come readily to me. As a teacher, I found it ever easier to empathize the author I taught than to pronounce a verdict. Yet I saw how treacherous to students and to myself that was. "But what, professor, do *you* think?" was a question from moral students; and if I turned from them, present before me in classroom or office, to the invisible presence over my shoulder of my old mentor, Babbitt, I met with the same question. These confrontations, and my own intellectual conscience, made requisite and necessary the taking of a stand.

Something should be said about the relation of teaching to criticism or, more generally, to writing. On this subject I have clear convictions. The best teachers I have known—the best as most rich and searching, germinal and fruitful—have been more than instructors of the young: they have, whether historical scholars or critics or poets, addressed themselves, through their published work, to their peers in kind; and this has given them an authority with their students which no mastery of pedagogic skill could impart.

In the way of understanding the nature of man and in the way of sustaining warmth, the relation with students has much to give the teacher; but sad is his lot if he is dependent on the admiration of his students, if he has no life except this vicarious life, if he has no work of his own, no continuing and intellectually sustaining work in progress.

The private psychic life of a literary man is precarious: some relatively objective and public continuum is necessary. The literary man, sensitive and impressionable, needs some firm skeletal structure of the kind provided by caste (status), creed (whether dogmatic or provisional), reputation (that last infirmity of noble minds), and work capable of relatively objective judgment by others. These, the classroom cannot provide.

My profession has been teaching—the teaching of literature—and whatever else I knew; my vocation has been writing—about literature and about life, of which literature is at once an imitation and a criticism. I have never been able with more than moderate success to integrate the two; have never learned how to prepare a course and have it turn into a book, or write a book and then dilate it into acceptable classroom performance. The two duties have had to coexist without much mutual traffic, courses starting from the interests and needs of students, books and essays from my own needs and interests. With me, it is the teaching which, by the process of adapting the product to consumers, disperses; and the writing, starting from an actual or desiderated self, which coheres and unifies. It is the writing which has kept me going and sustained me.

I generalize: the spiritual center and motivation of highest usefulness in one's profession is the finding of one's vocation.